Rupture

Manuel Castells

———————

Rupture

The Crisis of Liberal Democracy

Translated by Rosie Marteau

polity

Polity Press
65 Bridge Street
Cambridge CB2 1UR, UK

Polity Press
101 Station Landing
Suite 300
Medford, MA 02155, USA

ISBN-13: 978-1-5095-3199-8
ISBN-13: 978-1-5095-3200-1 (pb)

A catalogue record for this book is available from the British Library.

Typeset in 11 on 13 pt Sabon
by Fakenham Prepress Solutions, Fakenham, Norfolk NR21 8NL
Printed and bound in Great Britain by CPI Group (UK) Ltd, Croydon

The publisher has used its best endeavours to ensure that the URLs for external websites referred to in this book are correct and active at the time of going to press. However, the publisher has no responsibility for the websites and can make no guarantee that a site will remain live or that the content is or will remain appropriate.

Every effort has been made to trace all copyright holders, but if any have been overlooked the publisher will be pleased to include any necessary credits in any subsequent reprint or edition.

For further information on Polity, visit our website:
politybooks.com

To my grandson Gabriel Millan Castells who fights for justice and peace

CONTENTS

OUR WORLD, OUR LIVES

There are malignant winds blowing on this blue planet. Our lives are reeling in the maelstrom of multiple crises. An economic crisis that persists through labour insecurity and low wages. A fanatical terrorism that fractures human coexistence, feeds day-to-day fear and fuels restrictions on liberty in the name of security. A seemingly inexorable march towards our only home, Earth, becoming uninhabitable. The permanent threat of resorting to horrific wars as a way of dealing with conflicts. Rampant violence against women who dare to be themselves. A whole galaxy of communications dominated by lies, now known as post-truth. A transparent society in which we have all been turned into data. And a culture reduced to entertainment, built on stimulating our basest instincts and the commercialization of our demons.

Yet there is an even deeper crisis, which has devastating consequences on the (in)capability of dealing with the multiple crises that poison our lives: the rupture of the relationship between those who govern and the governed. The lack of trust in institutions, observed practically all over the world, delegitimizes political representation and so deprives us of a safe haven to protect us in the name of common interest. This isn't a question of political choices, of right or left. The rupture is more profound than that, on both an emotional and cognitive level. It is about the gradual collapse of a political model of representation and governance: liberal democracy, which had been established through blood, sweat and tears over the last two centuries as the antidote to authoritarian states and institutional despotism. Whether in the United States, Spain, Greece, Italy, Brazil, South Korea or many other countries, in recent years we have seen extensive grassroots mobilizations against the current system of party politics and parliamentary democracy under the slogan 'they don't represent us!' It's not about a rejection of democracy, but rather of liberal democracy as it exists in each country, in the name of 'real democracy' as the 15-M movement proclaimed it in Spain. This evocative term invites us to dream, debate and act, but also exceeds the confines of established institutions. Profoundly different types of political alternatives emerge from this rejection, which, in practice, challenge existing political institutions and seriously disrupt the national and global political order. Trump, Brexit, Le Pen, Macron (the political party pooper), Spain's Podemos, Greece's Syriza, Italy's Cinque Stelle Movement, in their ideological diversity, are all striking expressions of a post-liberal order – or chaos. So, too, is the total disintegration of the political system of Brazil, a key Latin American country; Mexico, victim to the narco-state; and post-Chavez Venezuela in a state of quasi-civil war. Or we could point to South Korean democracy, where the corrupt president Park Geun-hye was in thrall to the powers of the occultist leader Choi Soon-sil, leading to her being overthrown. Or there is the Philippine president who practises summary executions as a way of tackling security issues. While South Africa plunged into a deep crisis of legitimacy leading to the forced resignation of President Zuma. On the other hand, in some countries popular revolutions arose from such institutional crises, seeking to articulate a new relationship between parliamentary and social representation, notably in Bolivia and

Ecuador. In other areas of the world, in particular in China and Russia, authoritarian regimes established themselves as effective alternatives to liberal democracy, while the Middle East is governed either by theocracies (Iran, Saudi Arabia) or dictatorships (Egypt, Syria), apart from Israel which exists in a constant state of war with its occupied territories. In Europe, neofascist movements have sprung up in Poland, Hungary, Romania and Bulgaria, and even in Germany, as an identity-driven reaction against the European Union. Of course, we can always still console ourselves with the Scandinavian example of representative democracy, but only if we disregard the fact that xenophobic nationalist parties are partners in the governments of Finland and Norway, in coalition with the right, and that the Danish government is propped up by the parliamentary support of xenophobes.

This book looks at the causes and consequences of the rupture between citizens and governments, and at the mother of all crises: the crisis of liberal democracy, which was once the last hope for overcoming the historic catastrophes of wars and violence. I will not offer solutions, because I don't have them, and because they are specific to each country. But if the political crisis that I describe does have a global dimension, over and above the unique features of each society, it must surely be about the gradual collapse of a model of representation. A collapse which, as it escalates, would leave us without legitimate tools to resolve our major issues collectively, just at the very moment that the storm clouds gather over our lives.

1

THE CRISIS OF DEMOCRATIC LEGITIMACY: THEY DO NOT REPRESENT US

Once upon a time there was democracy

Democracy, Robert Escarpit once wrote, is when you hear knocking at your door at five in the morning and presume it's the milkman. Those of us who lived through Franco's Spain know the value of this minimalist version of democracy, one that is still not enjoyed by most of the planet. But after millennia of constructing institutions to which we, the people, can delegate the sovereign power that we theoretically hold, we're looking for something more. Indeed, this is what the model of liberal democracy purports to offer us, namely: respect for people's basic rights and the political rights of citizens, including the freedoms of association, assembly and speech, through the rule of law protected by the courts; the separation of powers between the executive, legislative and judiciary; free, periodic and verified choice over who holds the decision-making duties in each of those powers; submission of the state and all its machinery to those to whom the citizens have delegated power; the opportunity to revise and update the constitution in which the principles of democratic institutions are enshrined – and, of course, preventing economic or ideological powers from running public affairs by way of the hidden influence they have on the political system. However simple the model may seem, centuries of blood, sweat and tears were spilled for it to become a reality in institutional practice and social life – although we should still bear in mind the many deviations from the principles of representation to be found in the small print of the law and in the biased practices of members of parliament, judges and government officials. For example, there is almost no electoral law that applies the principle of 'one person, one vote' when it comes to the correspondence between the number of votes and the number of seats. The structure of judicial power depends indirectly or directly on the political system, including the courts which interpret constitutional principles. In reality, democracy is built around the very relationships of social power that founded it, and it adapts as those power relationships evolve, while privileging the power that is already crystallized within institutions. It cannot therefore be called representative, unless the large majority of citizens believe that they are being represented. The strength and stability of institutions depends on their inherent validity in people's minds. If the subjective link between what citizens think and want and the actions of those we elect and pay for is broken, this creates what we call a crisis of political legitimacy, namely, the widely-held feeling that the agents of the political system do not represent us. In theory, this imbalance corrects itself in liberal democracy through the plurality of options available, and periodic elections to choose between said options. In practice, choice is limited to those who are already embedded in institutions and in society's vested interests, with all sorts of obstacles in the way for anyone who tries to gain entry to this well-defined political domain. Indeed, the fundamental agents of politics, the parties, may well differ in terms of policies, but they agree on maintaining their monopoly on power within a pre-established framework of possibilities. Politics is professionalizing, and politicians are becoming a social group that defends its common interests above those of the people that it purports to represent: they make up a political class that, with honourable exceptions, transcends ideologies and protects its oligopoly. Furthermore, by their very nature parties undergo a process of internal bureaucratization, predicted by Robert Michels as far back as the 1920s, limiting their renewal to leadership contests and distancing themselves from any oversight or decision-making by their members. In fact, once the act of election is complete, dominated by electoral marketing and communications strategies involving very little debate and participation of members and the electorate, the system effectively goes on to function autonomously of citizens. Parties simply take the pulse of public opinion, and never bindingly, through polls strictly designed by the people who commission them. Even so, citizens will vote, elect and even become energized and mobilized around whomsoever they entrust with their hopes, shifting periodically whenever hope exceeds the fear of change that is the most basic emotional tactic in the maintenance of political power. And yet the recurrent letting down of those hopes begins to erode legitimacy, until resignation gives way to indignation when things become unbearable, such as when fraudulent banks are rescued from an economic crisis with taxpayers' money while essential services for people's lives are cut. We are promised that things will get better if we just hold on and keep swallowing things, and when this proves not to be the case, we must either choose to break away from everything, or just endure it all. Breaking away from institutions comes at a high personal and social cost, including being pilloried by the media, which is, after all, controlled either by financial interests or the state, despite the often heroic resistance of many journalists. At times of economic, social, institutional and moral crisis, people refuse to tolerate what they once accepted simply because there was no other choice. What was once a model of representation collapses into people's subjectivity. All that remains is the stark reality that this is just how things are, and that anyone who doesn't accept it is welcome to take to the streets, where the police will be waiting. That is the crisis of legitimacy.

This is what is happening across much of the world, including Europe and the United States. More than two-thirds of people on the planet think that politicians do not represent them, that the parties (all of them) prioritize their own interests, that the resulting parliaments are not representative and that governments are corrupt, unjust, bureaucratic and oppressive. In the almost unanimous perception of citizens, the most poorly viewed profession is that of a politician, and all the more so because they endlessly seem to reinvent themselves and rarely return to ordinary life as long as they can prosper among the winding little alleyways of institutional bureaucracy. This widely-held feeling of rejection of politics in its current form does differ in nature between countries and regions, but it is ubiquitous. Even in countries like the Scandinavian nations, where democratic virtue has been a hopeful reference point, public opinion has undergone the same trend for a while. I therefore take the liberty of referring the reader to the statistics and references from reliable sources that can be found on this book's website, to allow you to find your own examples from across the world. Having said all that, if this is broadly the situation on a global level, allowing for certain differences, perhaps it is simply the lot of any human institution, liberal democracy included. We often refer to Churchill's famous 1947 quotation, that 'democracy is the worst form of Government, except for all those other forms that have been tried from time to time'. Perhaps, but rather than engaging in a metaphysical debate about the very essence of democracy, what strikes me is that ever fewer people believe in this form of it, liberal democracy, while the great majority simultaneously continue to defend the democratic ideal. It is precisely because people want to believe in democracy that their sense of disillusionment in the way they experience it is even more profound. This disillusionment is giving rise to social and political behaviours that are transforming institutions and modes of governance everywhere, and it is this that I believe important to analyse. As for the inevitability of the perversion of the democratic ideal, it doesn't seem very useful to me to philosophize about how ill-fated human nature is, a stifling narrative that simply justifies continuity of the status quo. It is far more relevant to investigate some of the reasons why the gulf between representatives and the people they represent has widened in the last two decades, having reached the breaking point of the wholesale popular rejection of anyone in power, without distinction. This has been given the pejorative label of populism by the political establishment and mainstream media, because the behaviours do not conform to the preordained institutional channels for political change. In reality, collective emotions are like water: when they encounter a blockage in their natural flow they will open up new routes, often with torrential force, until they inundate the exclusive spaces held by the established order.

The roots of wrath

The crisis of liberal democracy is a result of the confluence of various mutually reinforcing processes. The globalization of the economy and of communication has eroded and deconstructed national economies and limited the capacity of the nation-state to respond within its own ambit to problems that are global in origin, such as financial crises, human rights issues, climate change, criminal financial networks or terrorism. The paradoxical thing is that nation-states were responsible for instigating the globalization process in the first place, by dismantling regulation and borders in the 1980s under Reagan and Thatcher, heads of the two countries leading the world economy at the time. These are the very same states that are now backpedalling, faced with the political impact on the sectors of society that have suffered the negative effects of globalization in every country. Meanwhile, professionals with better education and broader possibilities are connecting with one another across the planet to form new kinds of social classes. This separates the cosmopolitan elites who create value in the global marketplace from local workers, who are devalued by industrial off-shoring and relocation, displaced by technological change and left vulnerable through labour deregulation. The resulting social inequality between the value-makers and the devalued is the most significant disparity in recent history. It goes further than that; the unfettered logic of the market accentuates differences between capacities based on what is or is not useful to global capital networks, production and consumption, such that beyond mere inequality we are seeing real polarization, whereby the rich become richer, above all at the very apex of the pyramid, and the poor even poorer. This dynamic is played out both in national economies and on a global scale, such that despite hundreds of millions of people worldwide being lifted from poverty and integrated into new forms of industrialization to revitalize and broaden the global market, fragmentation within every society and between every country is becoming ever more acute. Until now, however, national governments – almost without exception – have chosen to hitch their wagons to globalization, to avoid being left behind from the new economy and the new distribution of power. To increase the competitive capacity of their countries, they created a new form of state: the network-state, based on the institutional articulation of nation-states, which do not disappear, but instead become nodes in a supra-national network in which sovereignty is partly surrendered in exchange for participation in managing globalization. This is clearly the case with the European Union, the boldest construct as a political response to globalization of the last half a century. However, the further nation-states distance themselves from the nations they represent, the more the state and the nation dissociate from one another. This leads to the crisis of legitimacy in the minds of many citizens, who are kept at the margins of the fundamental decisions that affect their lives, which are now taken elsewhere, outside of institutions of direct representation.

Added to this crisis of representation is an identity crisis borne of globalization. The less control people have over the market and their state, the more they retreat into a personal sense of identity which cannot be dissolved by the pace of global flows. They take refuge in their nation, their homeland, their god. While the triumphant elites of globalization proclaim themselves citizens of the world, broad social sectors hunker down into the cultural spaces, which feel familiar and where their value is dependent on their community, rather than just their bank balance. Social fracture is compounded by cultural fracture. The elites' scorn at people's fear of stepping outside of the local without guarantees of protection becomes a source of humiliation. This is where the seeds of xenophobia and intolerance are sown, in the growing suspicion that politicians are concerned with the rest of the world, but not them. The political identity of citizenship, built on statehood, is being replaced by diverse cultural identities that convey a meaning beyond the boundaries of the political.

The latent contradictions in the economy and society as transformed by globalization, the resistance of identity and the dissociation between state and nation, were all phenomena that became apparent in social practices during the economic crisis of 2008–10. Crises are moments that reveal the fault lines in a system and thus mediate between a society's underlying trends, the awareness of issues and the practices that emerge to alter trends which are perceived as damaging for people, despite being functional for the system. At the root of this crisis of political legitimacy is the financial crisis, which went on to become an economic and employment crisis, and which erupted in the United States and Europe in the autumn of 2008. In reality it was the crisis of a form of capitalism, global financial capitalism, a model based on the interdependence of world markets and on the use of digital technologies to create virtual speculative capital that imposed its dynamic of artificial value creation onto the productive capacity of goods and services. Indeed, this speculative spiral took down a substantial proportion of the financial system and was on the verge of generating an unprecedented catastrophe. Poised on the very edge of the precipice, governments – using our money – saved capitalism. Case in point: one of the institutions that quite literally went bust was AIG, the American insurance firm that insured most of the world's banks. If it had gone under like Lehman Brothers, it would have dragged the whole system down with it. The US government saved it (with the agreement of Obama who was president-elect at the time) by buying 80 per cent of its shares, a de facto nationalization. And so, one by one, national governments intervened, attesting to the fallacy of the neoliberal ideology that contends that state intervention in markets is harmful. In fact, risky speculative practices now assume no risk, because they know that major financial corporations will be bailed out where necessary, and their executives will continue to earn astronomical bonuses, including multimillion compensation payouts for changing jobs. Even when fraud is involved, they seem to come up untouched. Or so the executives of Bankia, a major bank, and many real estate companies in Spain believed, until they were hit by a wave of public indignation that swept across the whole nation.

The economic crisis and the policies that oversaw it in Europe were a key factor in the crisis of political legitimacy. Firstly, this was due to the sheer magnitude of the crisis, which spread from finance throughout industry as the flow of credit was shut down, above all for small and medium-sized enterprises, the main employers. Unemployment reached previously unprecedented levels, predominantly affecting young people. In Spain, hundreds of thousands of people were forced to emigrate, and those who did finally find work had to accept precarious conditions that saw their troubles prolonged indefinitely. Even more detrimental and revealing, however, were the austerity politics imposed by Germany and the European Commission, a German-style straitjacket that paid no attention to the individual conditions of each country. This set in motion the profound sense of mistrust towards the European Union as an institution, which seemed to be more an instrument of discipline than solidarity.

This feeling of injustice was heightened as financial holes originating from speculative activities and the abuse of those responsible for them were being plugged, with the consent of the Bank of Spain in Spain's case, alongside severe cuts to spending on health, education and research. The protecting state prioritized the protection of speculators and fraudsters over the needs of citizens who had been hit by the crisis and unemployment. Although Spain's case is particularly messy because Socialist leader Zapatero and Conservative leader Rajoy actually managed to change the country's sacrosanct constitution to reflect the diktat of Merkel and the European Commission in return for rescuing the banks and public debt, the same sorts of austerity practices were imposed right across Europe. This was not the response of the United States, where Obama's administration increased public spending, principally on infrastructure, education and innovation, allowing the country to recover from the crisis much more quickly than Europe. Meanwhile, in Europe the economic crisis undid the welfare state, with social democracy being complicit in policies that led to this next phase of the crisis. This austerity policy took its toll on public services in France, Germany, Scandinavia, UK, Netherlands, Greece, Portugal, Italy and Spain, where traditional left-wing voters felt betrayed, increasing the sense of political distrust in established parties.

Just as citizens in every country were being asked to make yet more sacrifices in the name of recovery from the crisis, in certain countries – and Spain in particular – the lid was lifted on a series of political corruption cases that served to utterly undermine trust in politicians and their parties. The scandals really racked up in the Spanish *Partido Popular* ('People's Party' or PP) camp, which entered government in November 2011 and took advantage of its political control over the justice system to try to halt corruption investigations at every level of the state. Despite their efforts, the professionalism of the police forces, including the Guardia Civil, ensured that a significant part of the systemic corruption consuming politics was still able to come to light, including the so-called Gürtel, Púnica and Lezo cases, among many others.

In every case, the illegal financing of the PP was tied up with the personal financial gain of leading party members and their intermediaries, particularly in the Madrid and Valencia regions where, according to the Guardia Civil, the PP had become a criminal organization to embezzle public funds and take bribes from companies. The corruption went beyond the PP, even reaching as far as the monarchy and triggering, in part, the abdication of King Juan Carlos, even though he was not personally implicated, while members of his family were. Systemic corruption was simultaneously uncovered in Jordi Pujol's Catalan nationalist party, in power for 23 years, which had set up a hidden kickback of 3–5 per cent on public works to benefit the party and some of its leaders, starting with the presidential household run by Marta Ferrusola, the Catalan President's wife. The *Partido Socialista Obrero Español* ('Spanish Socialist Workers' Party' or PSOE) was not innocent of corruption either, particularly in Andalusia, where the party's successful electoral machinery had been taking backhanders for years from fraudulent employment and training subsidies. The public's disgust with systemic political corruption was a determining factor in the failure of trust in their paid representatives, who were also raking in healthy bonuses by profiting from their positions and exploiting companies.

Although Spanish politics is among the most corrupt in Europe, political corruption is in the basic DNA of almost any political system, the USA and EU included, and one of the factors that has had the biggest part to play in the crisis of legitimacy. If the people responsible for enforcing the rules of coexistence within a society are not even following them themselves, how can we carry on delegating power to them and paying them our taxes? It is usually said that it is just a matter of a few rotten apples and that this should be expected given human nature. Yet with a handful of exceptions, such as Switzerland or Scandinavia (excluding Iceland), corruption is a systemic trait of contemporary politics. Perhaps it was ever thus, but the rise of liberal democracy in recent times ought to have diminished rather than increased it, as has apparently been the case according to studies by Transparency International. Why are we seeing this trend? In part it is due to the high cost of communications and media-driven politics, as I will examine shortly; legal party funding comes short of the actual cost of professional politics. It would, however, be difficult to increase the proportion of public funds allocated to parties, given the low opinion held of them by citizens. This is the catch 22: we should not pay any more to corrupt politicians, but politicians therefore turn to corruption to fund their activities and in some cases, pocket something for themselves in the process. But there is something deeper going on here. It is the ideology of consumption as value, and money as a measure of success that accompanies the triumphant neoliberal model centred on the individual and his or her immediately monetized satisfaction. Traditional ideologies, whether the egalitarian ideas of the left, or those that serve the values of the conventional right, have lost their way, and the quest for personal success through politics is now tied to the personal accumulation of capital by profiting from the period that positions of power are held. The cynical side of politics as manipulation eventually leads to a reward system aligned with the corporate world of profit, whereby politics is viewed as a business. In short, people aren't corrupt without being corrupted, and the practices of large companies the world over include buying favours from authorities that regulate or commission public services and public works. As many businesses decide, you have to be in it to win it. This is how boundaries between the economic and the political spheres become blurred, and how the proclaimed pre-eminence of politics serves to hide its very failings.

The self-destruction of institutional legitimacy by the political process

The struggle for power in contemporary democratic societies negotiates media politics and scandal politics, and the communicative autonomy of citizens. The digitalization of all data and the modal interconnection of messages have created a media universe in which we are all permanently immersed. Our construction of reality, and consequently

our behaviour and decisions, depend on the signals that
we receive and exchange within that universe. Politics is no
exception to this basic rule of living in the network society,
a society into which we have all dived headfirst. In practice,
the only politics that really exists is the politics we are
shown by the multimodal media world that has taken form
over the last two decades. In this world, media messaging
designed to form political opinions needs to be extremely
simple. The most succinct image to use is a human face,
onto which we project ourselves based on a relationship
of identification that builds trust. As the most currently
advanced neuroscience tells us, at its core, politics is fundamentally emotional, however much this might irritate the
rationalists holding on to a vision that has long since lost its
lustre. From this first emotional reflex that makes an imprint
on our visual and emotional universe, we then move on to
the cognitive process of working things out and making
decisions. Impressions start to be solidified as opinions,
which are corroborated or retracted as part of the continuous
debate that takes place on social networks, interacting with
news media. Mass communications are funnelled through
personal forms of mass self-communication, via the Internet
platforms that are ubiquitous in our lives. Because trust in
the positivity of a project is constructed around a person's
leadership potential, the dynamics of having to construct a
message that is simple and easily debatable in a multiform
universe leads to the personalization of politics. As such,
the most effective form of political attack is to destroy this
trust through the moral degradation of someone's character
and image as leader. Negative messages are five times more
effective in terms of influence than positive ones, so it becomes
about inserting negative content related to the image of the
person you want to destroy, in order to sever the ties of trust
with citizens. Hence the practice of professional political
operators, who go around searching for material that could
be damaging for certain political leaders, manipulating and
even fabricating it to increase its destructive impact. This is
the origin of scandal politics, as described and proposed by

the Cambridge sociologist John Thompson, which can now be found at the front and centre of political processes in every country. Now that everyone needs to be forewarned and prepared against insidious attacks, all politicians go around collecting ammunition – whether for offensive or defensive purposes – and end up playing the scandal politics game, obscuring more meaningful debate. In reality, studies show that this process is already so habitual that political victories and defeats no longer necessarily follow the course of scandals. People frequently end up preferring 'their own corrupt candidate' over his or her corrupt counterpart because given that they are all the same – according to the general perception – scandals can be disregarded, except for the case of political virgins who manage to hold on to their haloes for a while. But while the effects of scandal politics on specific politicians are indeterminate, the practice does have a devastating second-tier effect: it inspires a feeling of distrust and moral reprobation towards all politicians and politics as a whole, thus contributing to the crisis of legitimacy. In a world of digital networks that allow anyone to express themselves, there are no real rules other than personal agency and freedom of speech. This means that traditional checking and censuring mechanisms fall by the wayside, messages of all types form a powerful and polymorphic groundswell, bots multiply and spread memes and sound bites all around and the post-truth world, which the traditional media end up participating in, transforms uncertainty into the only reliable truth: 'my truth', each individual's truth. The fragmentation of messaging and the ambiguity of communication elicit unique and personal emotional responses, which are then constantly fuelled by hope-destroying tactics, ensuring that nothing changes. The main effect of this politico-digital cacophony is to cast doubt on anything that we cannot personally verify. The connection between the personal and the institutional breaks down. The circle closes in on itself. While we blindly search for the return of this mythical democracy that maybe once existed, somewhere, some time.

2

GLOBAL TERRORISM: THE POLITICS OF FEAR

Fear is the most powerful of human emotions. Indiscriminate terrorism taps into this, the kind of terrorism that kills, maims, injures, kidnaps and alienates anywhere and at any time, sowing seeds of fear in people's minds. Its effects on politics are profound, for wherever there is fear, the politics of fear will surely follow. This is the sort of politics that deliberately exploits people's obvious desire for protection to institute a state of permanent emergency, which can begin to corrode and in practice ultimately negate civil liberties and democratic institutions. Although terrorism, fear and politics have always formed a sinister *ménage à trois*, over the last two decades they have come to occupy the forefront of daily life to such an extent that many countries find themselves in a world where children are raised in a climate of fear, and one where citizens accept being watched and monitored electronically, searches when travelling, preventative detentions and the militarization of their public spaces. This is because these precautions are always for 'other people', for those whose ethnicity or religion makes them potential suspects. Gradually, exceptions for security reasons become the norms that govern our lives.

Terrorism has no ideology other than the exaltation of death, a martial mentality that has seen multiple incarnations. Spain suffered ETA and GAL (Grupos Antiterroristas de Liberación),[1] while there have been guerrilla fighters and paramilitaries in Colombia, criminal cartels and the narco-state in Mexico, Pinochet's death squads in Chile, and Palestinian and Israeli commandos in the Middle East – and so many others besides. But what has truly arrived on the global stage and transformed the political narrative is terrorism rooted in Islamic fundamentalism, and the counter-terrorism measures of nation-states that have turned the planet into a battlefield where for the most part civilians are the ones to die, particularly Muslim civilians. At the root of this form of terrorism lies the humiliation of many Muslims, disparaged by Western culture and oppressed by military dictatorships in hock to world powers, as explained by Edward Said in his book *Orientalism*. Its articulation as a form of combat was, however, the result of the efforts of the sorcerer's apprentices at the CIA, Mossad, Pakistan's Inter-Services Intelligence (ISI) agency and Saudi intelligence at the tail end of the Cold War. To overthrow the Soviet Union in Afghanistan, the United States, Pakistan and Saudi Arabia armed and organized Afghan warlords and recruited thousands of Islamic volunteers who were prepared to die in the fight against communist atheism. They were assembled in Pakistani training camps managed by an organization known as Al Qaeda ('the Base'), led by a profoundly religious Saudi intelligence agent who was a member of an eminent family responsible for conserving Islam's holy sites. His name: Osama Bin Laden. The strategy worked; the Soviets lost their first war in Afghanistan, like so many others who had tried and failed to conquer the country, and their influence and morale suffered a major blow. The United States had, however, underestimated the determination and aims of Bin Laden and his *mujahidin*. With the Soviet Union defeated,

---

[1] Translator's note: Antiterrorist Liberation Groups; state paramilitary death squads intended to fight ETA.

they turned their weapons towards the 'Great Satan'; if the United States were defeated, *jahiliyyah* (ignorance of God) would be eliminated from the world and the *ummah* (global community of believers in the true god) could at last come together. The task was arduous and long, an asymmetrical confrontation in which terrorism would be the key weapon because, in the words of Bin Laden, Islamic martyrs have no fear of death, while Westerners cling desperately to life. The tipping point was the audacious and brutal attack on the United States on 9/11, 2001: a day that changed the world forever. Bin Laden wanted to inspire in young Muslims the value of confronting the United States through direct action with a model attack on its power centres – and he achieved it. But he also intended to provoke the United States so that its soldiers would be sent to die in the sands of the desert and in the mountains of Afghanistan – and he achieved that too. He counted on the senseless cooperation of American neoconservative strategists and oil companies, who saw the chance to oust Saddam Hussein and impose their own control over the Middle East. Not so much for the oil, which they already have secured in the Arabian Peninsula and they could actually have obtained from Saddam Hussein himself, but rather to definitively assert their power over a crucial region in terms of the global economy and oil deals. Although Afghanistan was the source of the 9/11 attacks, the US response focused on occupying Iraq, based on the pretext of the scandalous fabrication of the existence of weapons of mass destruction. Bush, Blair and Aznar will go down in history as the irresponsible cynics who lit the touchpaper of war in Iraq that went on to spread across the entire Middle East. The invasion destabilized Iraq without being able to take control of it and exacerbated the secular conflict between Sunni and Shia Muslims, which had the paradoxical outcome of establishing a Shia government. As soon as US troops were forced to withdraw in light of the opposition to the war that helped bring Obama to the White House, this Shia government became allied with Iran and sustained by its militias. From the ruins of Iraq arose a new and formidable military terrorist organization, Islamic State, which unified Sunni military cadres from Saddam's regime, humiliated and imprisoned by the United States, with the remnants of Al-Qaeda in Iraq and Sunni tribes subjected to abuse by the Shia government. Islamic State was built up territorially, unlike Al-Qaeda, taking advantage of the power vacuum in Iraq and later Syria. In Syria, a democratic movement against the Assad dictatorship rose up in 2011, and was then manipulated and split up into factions by various powers. On the one side was Saudi Arabia, Jordan and Qatar, with an anti-Shia and anti-Iranian strategy. On the other was the United States trying to overthrow Assad, an ally of Russia and Iran. Assad's violent repression, supported militarily by Russia and the Iranian Revolutionary Guard, weakened democratic resistance and left the insurgents at the mercy of various Islamic militias, propped up by different states and Islamist networks. It was amongst this fracturing that Islamic State, led by Al Baghdadi, an Iraqi theologian tortured by the US at the infamous Abu Ghraib prison, achieved a series of military victories and established a caliphate with a global intent, with its capital in the Syrian city of Raqqa. The city resisted for a long time until it fell in 2017 to the combined assault of US and Russian bombardment, Assad's army, Syrian militias, the Kurdish Peshmerga, and the timely intervention of Turkey. The caliphate's example of power and its effective propaganda campaign and online recruitment attracted thousands of aspiring martyrs, young Muslims from across the world, but above all Europe. This is where a key connection was made, forming the basis of Islamic terrorism's dissemination in European societies, with decisive effects on the politics of Western democratic nations. The total breakdown of Iraq and Syria created millions of refugees, a consequence that combined with the bubbling over of contained rage felt by young European Muslims, who saw in the barbarity of Islamic State the chance for a purifying catharsis of their marginalized and oppressed existence, in which they felt their identity doubly negated both as Europeans and as

Muslims. Their actions shattered peaceful coexistence and led to a state of permanent alert across the whole of Europe, bringing with them a wave of xenophobia and Islamophobia that transformed the European political sphere.

The acts of terrorism that have occurred in major European cities since 2014 (and since 2004 in Spain) are the result of the meeting of three factors. Firstly, the marginalization and discrimination experienced by the nearly twenty million Muslims in the European Union in terms of employment, education, housing, politics and culture, more than half of whom were in fact born in Europe and yet are not recognized as such, while their religion is stigmatized on a daily basis by their fellow citizens. This is why most attacks take place in countries with the highest representation of Muslims in the population, such as France, Belgium, Germany or the United Kingdom. Not that other countries are immune from intense jihadist activity: we need only remember Barcelona and Cambrils in Catalonia. Secondly, there is the global jihad movement symbolized initially by Al-Qaeda and subsequently by Islamic State or Boko Haram in Africa, with its images on the internet that sustain, inform and occasionally connect up young Muslims in search of meaning, in Europe and worldwide. It is this search for meaning which seems to be the third and most significant motivating factor in radicalization, a personal process through which somebody progresses from rage and rebellion to the idea of martyrdom and on to committing a terrorist act. This activity is often conducted on an individual basis or with friends and relatives, but typically incited collectively through places of worship, images designed to indoctrinate and manipulate followers, internet chat rooms, Western prisons and trips to the promised lands of Islam at war. But what is this meaning, and where does the need to search for it come from?

The sociologist Farhad Khosrokhavar, the pre-eminent analyst of Islamic martyrdom, has interviewed hundreds of young people radicalized in French prisons. He found a systematic narrative describing the emptiness of life in the

West's rotten consumerist societies, the paucity of human relationships and the daily struggle to survive in a state of nihilism, and for nothing. Fundamentally, it is the sort of existential anguish that is typical of the youth of any society in crisis, but aggravated by the specific condition of not belonging to any country or any culture, until finding its home in this mythical idea of Islam, which encompasses every promise of subjectivity in a totalizing act, whereby sacrificing the mortal lends humanity meaning. It goes further than this, as Michel Wieviorka has shown: this search is not exclusive to Muslims, but in fact extends to many young Europeans of non-Muslim origins, who live lives equally devoid of meaning and who hope to find it in this mutated form of a purifying, religious absolute. Hence the thousands of Europeans, both men and women, who travel to die in Syria and who, if they manage to return to the place that never felt like home, continue to pursue their Islamic project and their terrorist radicalization. This is why global Islamic terrorism, which finds its most violent expressions in the Middle East, Asia and Africa, home to millions of Muslims, has become a permanent feature of our societies. Police and even military repression can punish and mitigate it, but it can't stop it. In fact, the more the Muslim community is stigmatized through preventative measures, the greater the fuel to foment the radicalization of its youth, with devastating effects on the practice of liberal democracy. In the collective imagination, a state of permanent emergency justifies the systematic restriction of civil and political liberties, creating a broad social breeding ground for Islamophobia, xenophobia and political authoritarianism. Perhaps this is the implicit objective of jihadist revolt: to expose the stark reality of liberal democracy's discrimination and political hypocrisy. This will allow the global religious community to triumph, whereby the sinful passions of colonial Christianity (the crusaders) are sublimated in an orgy of violence and cruelty from which we will re-emerge, purified by the actions and grace of the Islamic martyrs who sacrificed themselves to rescue humanity from its moral vacuum. This is the senselessness of this search for some sense, and it is also how liberal democracy, already weakened at its own hand, is being undermined by the enforced negation of its principles by the onslaught of terrorism.

3

THE REBELLION OF THE MASSES AND THE COLLAPSE OF POLITICAL ORDER

Globalization, anti-globalization and nationalism: rebellion of the masses

Fear of globalization leads people to seek refuge in the idea of the nation. Fear of terrorism persuades them to turn to the state for protection. Multiculturalism and immigration, essential aspects of globalization, prompt them to appeal to their communal identity. In this context, distrust in parties and institutions that were founded on the basis of the values and interests of another era, leads people to search for new political actors to believe in. It is invariably the most vulnerable sections of society that react, moved by fear, the most powerful of all emotions. They then mobilize around those who are prepared to say whatever is censored in elite discourse; to those who articulate a xenophobic and racist narrative, without beating around the bush; to those who call for state force as a way of resolving threats; to those who distil problems down to the simple opposition between rich and poor; and to those who denounce the prevailing climate of corruption, even though in many cases they are part of that very corruption.

This is how the crisis of democratic legitimacy has led to the generation of a discourse of fear and to political ideologies that propose going back to the drawing board. Back to the state as the decision-making centre, over economic oligarchies and global networks. Back to the nation as cultural community, to the exclusion of anyone who does not share the values of those defined as 'native'. Back to race, as the natural frontier of the ancestral right of the majority ethnic group. Back, too, to the patriarchal family unit, as the primary institution of daily protection against a world in chaos. Back to God, as foundation. This leads to institutions of coexistence being rebuilt on these pillars, inherited from history and now threatened by the multidimensional transformation of the global economy, social networks, cultural fusion and politics of partisan bureaucracies. This reconstruction process stems from a sense of affirmation, embodied in a leader or a cause that arises in opposition to the delegitimized institutions of the establishment. The new legitimacy functions through opposition and is constructed around a discourse that proposes an overall rejection of the status quo. It promises salvation through a rupture with the deep-rooted institutional order and with the culture of the cosmopolitan elites, suspected of dismantling the tribe's last defences against the invasion of the unknown.

This is the common thread running through the diverse protests and developments transforming the established political order in different countries. We find it in the improbable rise to power of a character as bizarre, narcissistic and vulgar as Trump to the imperial office of President of the United States. We find it in the unthinkable secession of the United Kingdom from the European Union, and in the extreme nationalist tensions that threaten to destroy the entire construct of the union. We find it in the sudden disintegration of France's political system, with the destruction of parties that had dominated the French and European political scene for half a century. We find it in the emergence of a political alternative in Italy, particularly represented by the Cinque Stelle Movement, coming to govern the country in May 2018 in alliance with the right-wing Lega Nord, both parties arguing for renegotiation of the fundamental principles of the European Union, and even EU membership, to increase national autonomy and the control that citizens have over their governments. And, albeit in different forms and with contradictory values, there are also elements of this anti-systemic rejection in the appearance of Syriza as the predominant party in Greece, in the triumph of the extreme right in Austrian elections and in the transformation of the Spanish political system inherited from the post-Franco democratic transition, under the impulse of new parties, Podemos and Ciudadanos. My intention is not to blend and confuse all of these various movements and individuals into one misleading amalgam. The emergence of new political agents with alternative, progressive values such as Syriza in Greece, the Bloco d'Esquerda in Portugal or Podemos and its coalitions in Spain, arising out of social movements against the crisis and against the state monopoly through two-party politics, is radically different from the xenophobic and ultra-nationalist expressions found in other countries. It does, however, form part of a wider and more profound movement of mass rebellion against the established order. This rebellion therefore needs to be analysed in all its diversity, taking into consideration each country's specific circumstances, while simultaneously tracing the common factors that underlie the rupture with the liberal political order.

Trump: the fruits of wrath

How could this happen? How could a rude and vulgar billionaire be elected to the most powerful presidency in the world, a property speculator mired in dirty deals, ignorant of international politics, dismissive about the conservation of the planet, a radical nationalist who is openly sexist, xenophobic and racist? Well, precisely because he is those things. Millions of people recognized themselves in his discourse and his persona, transcending political parties, people whose voices had been silenced by the 'political correctness' of the cosmopolitan elite that had come to monopolize the country's politics, culture and economy. But before we go jumping to the conclusion that Americans are a herd of racists, let us not forget that in the two previous elections they had elected a black, progressive president. So what happened? What changed in US society and politics? Analysis of the improbable rise of Donald Trump to the apex of American – and thus world – power is key if we are to fathom the depths of the crisis of liberal democracy and determine its consequences.

How it happened: the 2016 electoral campaign
When Trump, who had been a member of the Democratic Party, announced he would be running for the Republican presidential primary nomination, few people considered him a genuine contender. To start with, the party was openly hostile to him – and the feeling was mutual. From the very outset, Trump positioned himself above the political establishment, Republican and Democrat alike, and addressed the public directly. He didn't need money; he was already rolling in it, and the rejection of his own party actually helped him in his strategy of appearing free from any previous ties. In February 2016, just before starting the Iowa primary campaign, he didn't have the support of a single governor or congressman. Between them, Jeb Bush, Ted Cruz and Marco Rubio divided up the sympathies of the various Republican factions, including the Tea Party populists, who supported Cruz and Rubio. In total, twelve candidates ran for the primaries – and Trump beat them all soundly when it came to votes. Despite substantial political and financial support, the Republican elite's main candidate and the next successor to the Bush dynasty, was forced to pull out of the running, leaving the field open to the populist and xenophobic nationalism shared by Trump, Cruz and Rubio, flanked by the largely irrelevant moderate, Kasich. Trump took the upper hand over all of them by opening his campaign with a direct attack on immigration and condemning Mexicans as thieves, rapists and drug traffickers. He expressed his xenophobia symbolically with the promise of building an impenetrable wall along the entire length of the border with Mexico, a powerful image that stirred up the imaginations

of those fearful of immigration. Effectively, he dared to take xenophobic logic to its very nadir, voicing out loud what many were thinking. Nor did he hold back from insulting Carly Fiorina, the only female candidate, and ridiculing his opponents. When his offensive opinions about women were made public, his zealous supporters – both male and female – dismissed them as jokes, while to the exponents of the machismo dominant in so many areas, they sounded like masculine liberation. To top it all, Trump called out globalization as the enemy of the people, echoing a feeling that was, especially amongst workers, widely held, plus he even had the gall to hold his Wall Street financial buddies accountable for people's economic hardship. By adding to this an anti-interventionist stance, based on the premise of not wasting American lives on defending people who don't deserve them, he paradoxically came closer to the traditional discourse of the left: anti-globalization and anti-war. Having completely shamelessly espoused all the various sources of popular dissatisfaction, on 24 May 2016, and with hardly any opposition, Trump had obtained enough delegates to secure the nomination at the Republican National Convention. Even then the Republican machinery tried to find a way to block him, out of fear of a catastrophic result in the presidential election. They disagreed with his programme of economic and political isolationism, but they didn't dare to confront Trumpism's militant followers, who were already fanatical.

So it was that the moment of truth arrived between Trump and Hillary Clinton. The Democrats' tactical mistake was to pitch another Clinton, closely linked to the political and financial establishment, against an anti-establishment candidate. Some observers suggest that Bernie Sanders, the democratic socialist senator from Vermont who represented a left-wing anti-establishment movement and whose election bid was openly sabotaged by the Democratic National Committee during the Democratic Primaries, would have achieved a better result than Clinton, boosted by the mobilization of young people. Young people who, without their candidate, abstained from voting for Hillary in a proportion significant enough to go some way towards explaining her defeat. Even young women did not see themselves represented by a candidate so closely associated with Wall Street. Despite all this, at the beginning of the campaign, Clinton had a clear advantage thanks to Trump's negative image among most women and ethnic minorities. Even so, Trump didn't bother setting up campaign offices in every state or trying to win politicians to his cause; Clinton brought in billions of dollars, twice the funds raised by Trump, and she also had twice as many campaign offices. But Trump led a movement. His relationship with the electorate was direct, at mass rallies with incendiary speeches. He adopted a fundamentally media-based strategy, understanding right from the primaries how to ensure permanent media coverage, without spending any money. He made scandalous and outrageous statements that were amplified by social networks and which the media felt under pressure to report, typically in a critical way. Thanks to his own media experience, Trump knew that it was essential to be in the media spotlight and above all on television, even if the coverage was negative. It was this constant presence that monopolized the debate and ensured discussions centred on him, his persona, what people were saying about him and how he was responding. His pathologically narcissistic personality managed to ensure that they weren't talking about his content or even about Hillary, but about him. The whole campaign revolved around Trump, his simple and reductive messaging and the weak and predictable response from Clinton. She won the TV debates (partly thanks to the support of journalists infuriated by Trump), but she lost presence on the public stage. More than this: Clinton's campaign was truly terrible, littered with some major, cardinal errors. For example, she wasn't able to temper herself from describing Trump's supporters as 'deplorable', which is precisely what the elite think of the less-educated classes. Nor could she ever get over the error of having sent thousands of emails from her personal account as Secretary of State. The little-known reason for this is that Hillary only used her BlackBerry because she couldn't manage more sophisticated and encrypted networks. But it was symptomatic of an arrogant attitude that, for the second time in an election campaign, led her to see herself as the natural victor because of her intellectual capacity. An intellect which is not in doubt, but which becomes a negative trait when it gives out an image of superiority over ordinary people – so much so, in fact, that not even the majority of white women would vote for her: 52 per cent of them voted for Trump.

However, there is no doubt that Clinton's electoral chances were seriously affected by the hacking of the Democratic National Committee's computers and by the interception of her private emails by the Russian government – via intermediaries – as reported by various media sources, which handed crucial information to Trump's campaign. Moreover, Russian intervention in the election, clearly geared to help Trump, also took the form of a major campaign of misinformation about Clinton and pro-Trump mobilization conducted in the Internet-based social networks by multiple hackers and thousands of robots. Yet, the manipulation of social network chats and messages was not the exclusive domain of Russian hackers. Most of these targeted campaigns were undertaken by Trump supporters themselves, using data sold by Internet companies, such as Facebook, to companies such as Cambridge Analytica, contracted by Bannon, strategist of Trump, to shape political opinion on social media. Facebook has acknowledged that it provided the data of 87 million of their users to companies that developed algorithms to customize messages to specific audiences and even individuals to be used in the campaign. In other words, the Russian intervention in the social media space was simply a component of a much broader effort of misinformation planned by Trump's campaign. More significant in terms of the role of Russian-commissioned hackers was the retrieval of confidential information from the Democratic Party and from Hillary Clinton herself, and the diffusion of this content by different means, including by the intermediary of Wikileaks.

On the subject of the Russian government's role in the presidential campaign in the US, it is worth pausing to reflect on the tactics deployed by Russian intelligence as part of a wider policy of destabilizing Western democracies, which gambled on Trump winning the election and sowing seeds of division in America. A dossier came to light after the election was over, published by the alternative news website Buzzfeed in January 2017. It had been written by an ex-MI6 British spy in Moscow, Christopher Steele, on behalf of the political research company Fusion GPS, in turn commissioned by a rich Republican enemy of Bush and by the Democratic National Committee. The report's aim was to prove the connection between Russian agents and the Trump campaign. Its first port of call was Trump's 2013 visit to Moscow, ostensibly to attend the Miss Universe contest, which he owned at the time. This trip allowed him to come into direct contact with high-level oligarchs including Algaramov, a property magnate of significant interest to Trump and a personal friend of Putin's, although Trump didn't manage to meet with Putin on this occasion. According to the dossier, the FSB (the Russian Federal Security Service) filmed Trump at the Ritz Carlton taking part in an orgy with prostitutes in the very same room as the Obamas had stayed, and that the women urinated in the Obamas' bed to gratify Trump. It seems that Putin later gave an order preventing this material from being used and fired those behind the set-up – but the recording remained, potentially to be used later if needed. This aside, the directly political connections between Russia and Trump's entourage dated from the beginning of his presidential election campaign, although they harked back to business dealings he had pursued in Russia since 2008. He hadn't really been interested in investing in Russia, but rather in courting Russian oligarchs to invest in his own property developments in the United States at a time when he was in serious financial difficulties. In this context, the really significant thing as described by Luke Harding, author of the best book on the Trump–Russia conspiracy (*Collusion*, 2017), is that every one of the 'president's men' behind his campaign had strong links to Russian oligarchs, Russian politicians and pro-Russian Ukrainians. Specifically, Trump's first campaign manager Paul Manafort made his fortune as an agent for pro-Russian Ukrainians in the United States, with a political consultancy that lobbied on behalf of the ex-president Yanukovych and against sanctions placed on Russia for the annexation of Crimea. He was supported by his deputy campaign manager Richard Gates, both of whom had lucrative business interests in Ukraine. Trump's foreign policy adviser Carter Page was an ex-Navy intelligence office with a PhD from London's SOAS (School of Oriental and African Studies), who did well for himself as a strategic consultant in the energy sector, consulting to Gazprom in Moscow and later forming an energy-related company in New York with Sergei Yatsenko, a Gazprom associate. Page regularly published papers in English-language academic journals in support of Russian policy on the Crimea. In July 2016, at the very height of the presidential campaign, Page was sent to Moscow where he spoke at a conference and met with Igor Sechin, a man who had Putin's utmost trust since their days in the KGB. Sechin was named chairman of Rosneft, Russia's main oil company. He was looking for a good link to Trump to forge an energy deal, and he found an excellent one in Page. Some time previously, Rosneft had collaborated with Exxon to develop a major gas exploration project in Sakhalin. Exxon's president at the time was Rex Tillerson, to whom Putin awarded the Russian Order of Friendship. Tillerson joined Trump's campaign and was appointed Secretary of State by Trump's administration, although he was dismissed in March 2018 because of his moderate standing in the conduct of foreign policy. The first National Security adviser to Trump's presidency was General Michael Flynn, who was forced to resign after just three weeks in the White House after admitting that he had lied to the FBI about money he had received from both Russia and Turkey. Flynn had been invited to Moscow before the election and had been to dinner with Putin, where they were photographed together. He gave an interview to Russia

Today in which he spoke in glowing terms about Russian policy in Europe. Page was replaced in the Trump team by a young international policy adviser, George Papadopoulos, who also acknowledged having had unauthorized contact with Russian intelligence and who is being indicted by the Special Prosecutor appointed by the US Attorney General to investigate the Russian interference in the Presidential election. Trump's personal lawyer, Michael Cohen, who has Ukrainian family and business ties, worked in New York real estate with Felix Sater and Jared Kushner, Trump's son-in-law, as well as on the unrealized project to build a Trump Tower in Moscow. Sater was part of the Russian mafia in New York, who turned FBI informant to avoid jail. Every single one of these figures has corroborated their Russian contacts and, with the exception of Tillerson, they have all been investigated by Special Counsel Robert Mueller and prosecuted for lying to the FBI. But the most important piece of evidence of the Russian connection dates back to a meeting held in a room at Trump Tower on 9 June 2016, at the initiative of the lawyer Natalia Veselnitskaya, who later confessed to be an informer for the Kremlin. Via the publicist Rob Goldstone, agent to Algaramov's son, Veselnitskaya offered Donald Trump Jr. potentially harmful information about Hillary in exchange for the promise of lifting sanctions against various Russian leaders if Trump became president. Trump Jr. replied that he loved the idea, but that it all depended on the value of the information. So it was that they all met in this room: Trump Jr., Jared Kushner (Trump's son-in-law), Manafort, Rob Goldstone, Emin Algaramov, Rivat Akmetshin (Russian counter-intelligence and lobbyist resident in Washington) and the mysterious lawyer herself. According to all the attendees, no such information was forthcoming, and the meeting came to an end without a deal. Nevertheless, forty minutes after the meeting, Donald Trump – who was at the Tower but did not attend the meeting in person – sent a detailed tweet describing Hillary Clinton's intercepted emails, fanning the flames of the accusations against her.

Ultimately, the outcome of this revelation was that shortly after the election, the FBI director James Comey took the decision to reopen the investigation into the content of Hillary's emails and their potential risk to national security. There is no doubt that this fact, and the very existence of the emails themselves for that matter, likely to have been obtained by hackers working for Russian intelligence stationed in Bulgaria and Romania, did have an impact on the election result. This is backed up by the exit polls from the day of the election, which can be found on the website that accompanies this book. That said, Comey's actions were not part of a conspiracy, but were prompted by his independent professionalism. This explains why Trump fired him after having benefited from his Clinton investigation, because alongside the information on Clinton, the FBI had also been gathering other data that would be damaging to Trump, related to his dealings with Russian banks and property firms.

While the Trump campaign's Russian connection is of huge interest on a geopolitical level, it was not, however, the determining factor in the result of the election, although it did contribute to the discrediting of Clinton.

Technically speaking, Clinton lost the election because white people voted in their droves for Trump, while African Americans, Hispanic and young people did not vote for her to the same degree as they had for Obama. This was largely down to Clinton's ambiguous attitude on issues as sensitive as the killings of black people by the police, where she expressed generic support for uniformed officers. Nevertheless, she did win the popular vote by more than two million votes, but the historically obsolete US Electoral College system gave Trump a comfortable margin of victory thanks to his support being concentrated in strategic Midwest states and Florida, along with his definitive superiority in rural areas and smaller cities: those forgotten by the system. Trump was elected by these forgotten people, who Hillary, in a revealing slip, had labelled the 'deplorables'.

Who voted for Trump: White America

At the beginning of the electoral campaign, Clinton and
Trump were the candidates with the most negative approval
ratings in the history of presidential elections. One third of
citizens had an unfavourable opinion of Clinton, and 40 per
cent felt the same way about Trump. The election was being
decided on the basis of the mobilization differential between
the candidates over the course of the campaign. While
support for Clinton was largely a reaction against Trump,
the Republican candidate did have the enthusiastic support
of a core electorate – first and foremost, white people.
Clinton lost the white vote to Trump by 21 percentage
points; Obama also lost this segment, but only by 12 points.
The Democrats' tendency to rely on the minority vote
became more and more pronounced as elections went on,
and culminated in a genuine mobilization of white people
of all classes and ages in favour of Trump. This trend was
particularly acute among the less-educated sectors (generi-
cally described as the 'working class'), where the vote was
67 per cent for Trump and 28 per cent for Clinton. However,
Trump was also successful with university-educated white
voters, winning by 49 per cent to Clinton's 45 per cent.
Even among white women, 58 per cent of those with a
lower education level voted for Trump. This racial difference
was decisive in the Midwestern states, so key to winning
the election because they are home to 40 per cent of the
electorate, where Trump won by a ratio of two votes
to one. In Pennsylvania, Clinton scored seven percentage
points lower than Obama in the previous election, eight in
Wisconsin, ten in Michigan, eleven in Ohio and fifteen in
Iowa, in the very heartland of industrial America that was
traditionally a Democrat stronghold. This is the source of
the widely expressed view that the white working classes,
hit by globalization and resentful of immigration, were the
agents of Trump's victory – but this is only part of the truth.
Exit polls do show that a negative attitude towards international trade correlates strongly with the Trump vote. But in
reality it was the entirety of white voters, transcending social

class, who turned out against Clinton. The female vote only just swung for Hillary in the highest social strata (i.e. college educated) and most significantly, among minorities. Ethnic minorities were the only groups that were clearly lost by Trump, and although the majority of young people voted for Clinton, they didn't do so in the same volumes as they had for Obama, due to their rejection of the establishment she represented. The territorial division of the vote was even more significant: Hillary won by 13 million votes in the 100 most populated urban areas, with the largest concentration of ethnic minorities, while Trump won by 12 million votes in the 3,000 remaining counties, or rather, in white, rural America, where he gained vote share of over 75 per cent. This explains why the Democrat vote in the big cities of the Midwest could not compensate for the wave of white rural voters, representative of the original resident white population, who supported the candidate that gave them hope about resisting the invasion of their country from above (globalization) and from below (immigration). The vote was cast by people who felt like, to use Arlie Hochschild's phrase, 'strangers in their own land'. A sense of racial belonging was the key indicator of this mass reaction among white people. It seems as though Obama's election, rather than having moderated and pacified racism, had actually incentivized it, handing Trump the white racial resentment vote. This was particularly accentuated among white people of a lower education level, but still noticeable among middle-class professional men – and was most pronounced of all among older white men. Studies did show a direct correlation between racist attitudes and the Trump vote, but although racists voted for Trump, the majority of Trump voters are not racist. They are people who feel threatened by their country's rapid economic, technological, ethnic and cultural change. This is why older white men supported Trump: they were trying to preserve their world, a world they saw disappearing day by day, where immigration was the most visible sign that their neighbours were no longer who they used to be. Furthermore, social class delineated the white vote – the higher a person's education level and economic status, the more likely they were to vote for Clinton, while Trump absolutely steamrollered the white vote amongst the working class, poorer rural areas and the regions in economic crisis. To put it another way, Trump did extremely well with voters that some analysts have called 'white trash', the pejorative epithet frequently used to describe poor white people throughout history. It was a cry for survival based on the only thing they had a handle on: being white American citizens, taking solace in their Bible, their nation and their guns. They wanted to stop the foreign invasion and defend their jobs against the rapacious spread of multinationals and bankers.

In summary, ethnic minorities, young people, educated women and big cities were Hillary's major backers, while the white, lower-educated sectors of society (men and women, old and young), industrial white workers, educated white men, white rural areas and all majority white areas voted overwhelmingly for Trump. It was white people, overall, who elected Trump, sending an explicit message about defending their identity and rejecting those who would dilute it through ethnic diversity.

Trump: an identity movement

The Trump vote has been associated with the economic discontent caused by the financial crisis and unemployment, and likened to similar reactions in Europe. It is true that workers' wages went down in real terms while professionals saw their salaries increase substantially, such that Trump's election was not so much a response to the financial crisis itself, as the social inequality exacerbated by policies intended to manage it. It is also true that industrial delocalization connected to globalization and the transformation of employment through automation did hit some workers in traditional industries, particularly the automotive, steel and metalwork sectors based primarily in the Midwest, along with coal mining. Since the year 2000, seven million industrial jobs have been lost, while 25 million have been created in service-based sectors. At the time of the election, however, thanks to Obama's expansive economic policy, the unemployment rate sat at just 5 per cent, its lowest level since 2005. It was admittedly much higher in the industrial regions at around 8 or 9 per cent, and a little higher among young people, but even so, the situation cannot be described as a profound crisis of living standards that could have led to such a broad and radical mobilization as the one that swept Trump to power. This had already been the case with Obama's election. In Trump's case, the explanation appears to point more to the cultural crisis of alienated populations, which began with the social disintegration of traditional working-class communities affected by industrial restructuring. In his emotive work *Hillbilly Elegy: A Memoir of a Family and Culture in Crisis* (2016), J.D. Vance describes his own experience among dysfunctional families living at the very edge of survival in Appalachian towns, and their continuing marginalization after emigrating to Ohio's industrial cities, where they were followed by the stigma of ignorance and violence. They face down this stigma with the pride of being exactly who they are, despite the disdain of the professional, educated groups who maintain control over all of American society's resources. Their sense of hatred for the elites extends to the immigrants that populate the country, with whom they compete for jobs and public assistance. Add to this the fact that they are faced with Wall Street-led globalization which they see as responsible for job losses, and it's not hard to see why the nation of America, with all its attributes, becomes the last bastion of hope and identity, in which they take refuge and solace.

In an extraordinary article in *Foreign Affairs* in April 2017, the historian Walter Russell Mead likened the movement around Trump to the populist Jacksonian revolt in the early nineteenth century. Faced with the internationalist ambitions of some of the Fathers of the Nation including Hamilton, President Andrew Jackson's followers insisted on the priority of defending white American citizens and preserving the principles of community values, freedom and equality, the characteristics of the new nation. This ideological current, in direct opposition to liberalism and global interventionism, has been maintained throughout US history and reignited whenever the financial and political elites put forward a cosmopolitan discourse that left 'true Americans' feeling excluded. Under Trump, this latent movement was expressed in different forms, from the attack on undocumented immigrants to the defence of the right to bear arms (to resist and overthrow the potential of government tyranny), and in the unconditional support for the police, criticized by the Black Lives Matter movement against racist repression. This neo-Jacksonism was based on an objection to globalization and a savage critique of the cosmopolitan nature and intellectual tolerance of the influential academic, financial and media sectors of the large urban population centres, particularly in California and New York. It also extended to the condemnation of the Washington-based political class, symbolic of the illegitimate government, and distanced from common people.

One possible explanation for the strength of the nationalist movement is the importance that identity politics has assumed in the United States, and the rest of the world. Many ethnic and cultural groups (African Americans, Hispanics, Mexicans, Native Americans, Asians of various nations and ethnicities, women, lesbians, gays, transsexuals and many other groups) have asserted their specific identity and fought for their rights. Suddenly, white men found themselves in a situation where no one was talking about their identity. It was even more than that: other identities were defining themselves in opposition to the supposedly dominant patriarchal identity of the white man, and their alpha identity was now being overtaken and negated. This sense of exclusion from predominant cultural expressions and protected categories with seemingly special rights gave rise to a need for those who were left behind by identity politics to stand up: white men.

This fertile breeding ground allowed racist, neo-Nazi and anti-Semitic groups who had long been lurking in the shadows to seize their moment and flourish. They came together under the banner of the *alt-right* and began to influence Trump's campaign through their presence in xenophobic media sources with an increasingly prominent standing among nativist Americans. One such source was Breitbart News, partially funded by the ultra-conservative billionaire Robert Mercer, who is very close to Trump. The executive director of Breitbart News, Steve Bannon, made a connection with Trump and went on to direct the final phase of his campaign from August 2016. Before we make an obligatory stop to examine this particular individual, it is worth emphasizing that the identity-driven nationalist movement that surrounds Trump is by no means racist or neo-Nazi in nature, although it does house racists such as the Ku Klux Klan and others. It has deep roots in the sense of personal humiliation and social marginalization felt by broad sections of society, a marginalization that began as labour displacement through the restructuring of the economy and which was drawn out, with terrible conse-quences, into the national opioid epidemic that is currently wreaking such havoc. The researcher Melina Sherman has studied the subject and shown that the roots of this epidemic lie in the vast numbers of desperate people who resort to legally prescribed opioid painkillers to escape their distress. This combines with pharmaceutical companies manipulating the quasi-legal market to meet this huge demand. More Americans have died from overdoses in this epidemic than in World War I and World War II together. The areas where the epidemic is the most acute overlap strongly with areas that voted for Trump. This isn't to draw the conclusion that drug addicts elected Trump, but that the cultural alienation and social marginalization of poorer sections of society simultaneously led people to disconnect through drug use, and to reconnect with Trump as their providential saviour.

Despite the fact that the alt-right was not dominant in the broadest popular movement that formed around Trump, some of its leaders did play a decisive role in the

ideology and politics of Trumpism, thanks to their direct
influence on Trump himself. This was particularly the case
with Steve Bannon, an ex-Marine, Harvard graduate, rich
Hollywood media impresario and radio and TV executive.
He had a vision to create a popular movement that could
stay in power through a policy of infrastructure that would
provide jobs reserved for the white American working
classes, combined with systematic opposition to immigration
and an institutional Islamophobia that would put national
security at the very centre of politics, in direct contrast to
the globalizing elites. He was made Trump's special adviser
at the White House and was even given a key post at the
National Security Council – until, that is, his confronta-
tions with various directors of the presidential cabinet and
members of the Trump family led to his dismissal in August
2017. The truth was that Trump's narcissism could not
stand Bannon being credited as the strategic architect of the
movement. Even out of the White House, however, Bannon
and his circle continue to have a major influence on the
national-populist movement that makes up the central core
of Trump's support. Ironically, it was Bannon who gave
the journalist Michael Wolff access to the White House to
conduct the interviews that formed the basis of his book *Fire
and Fury*, released in January 2018 despite the president's
best efforts to block its publication. The book documents
the organizational and political chaos of Trump's entourage,
asserting that many of the president's colleagues consider him
to be unpredictable and psychologically unstable. Trump's
presidency is a defining element of the chaotic maelstrom
currently engulfing liberal democracy.

*Trump against the world: a dysfunctional White House
under siege*
The presidency's baptism of fire revealed the true Trump.
Like so many US presidents before him, he gave in to the
might of Wall Street, which he had vilified so vociferously
during his campaign. The key economic post of Secretary of
the Treasury was given to ex-Goldman Sachs banker Steven

Mnuchin, following a long presidential tradition that assures this company a definitive hold over the twin reins of US political and financial power. He rode the wave of economic progress that Obama had instigated with his policies of increased public spending and technological innovation, which allowed Trump to boast about a significant rise in the stock market in spite of reservations expressed by the business community about his ideology. He also massively reduced taxes for corporations and the wealthy, creating genuine euphoria in business circles. In other policy areas, however, he did not stray far from his electoral promises: he tried to repeal Obama's health reform; he pressured car companies into not relocating to Mexico and tried to ban residents of some Muslim countries from entering the US, equating a country having Islam as its major religion to a national security risk. He toughened anti-immigrant policies, condoned police repression of minorities and protected and 'understood' the racist groups of the alt-right. He also pushed on (albeit with difficulty) with his plan to build his disgraceful wall along the Mexican border. He voided the primary multilateral trade treaties, in particular the Pacific, North American and Latin American agreements, and announced the withdrawal of the United States from the Paris Agreement on climate change. As if that wasn't enough, he confronted and, in some cases, insulted various European political leaders (although he went doe-eyed over Macron), threatened to start a war with North Korea, withdrew from the Nuclear Deal with Iran, hinted at military intervention in Venezuela and returned to a state of cold war with Cuba, despite having made illegal business deals on the island in the past. Although he toyed with the idea of a trade war with China, he proceeded with caution because he realized that Xi Jinping was too important to face head-on. On the other hand, his renowned admiration for Putin didn't materialize in changes to strategic alliances, as suspicions surrounding Russian intervention in the electoral campaign continued to define the course of his political destiny. Nevertheless, he refrained from implementing the new sanctions on Russia that had been voted for by Congress in reprisal for the country's interference in the election.

He did, however, come up against five sources of opposition that derailed some of his initiatives and limited his ambitions, the first being the almost unanimous criticism of the media. In Bannon's eyes, the media were the only political enemy they really had to contend with, and Trump systematically tore into and belittled them. The second was the judiciary, which clearly demonstrated its independence by opposing the president's unconstitutional actions. In this case too, Trump responded by turning his army of followers against the judges. Then came the FBI reasserting its independence, and although its director Comey paid for his temerity with removal from office and unfavourable retirement, the agency continued to investigate Trump's entourage under their new director. Similarly, the naming of a Special Counsel to investigate the relationship between Russia and Trump's campaign showed that even his own Attorney General Jeff Sessions could not eschew his institutional duty when it came to the president. Last of all was Congress, including many Republicans, which became alarmed by Trump's threats of going beyond the limitations of presidential power and slowed down a range of initiatives, including health reform, the building of the wall and the mass expulsion of the so-called 'dreamers', who had arrived illegally on US soil as children. When Trump railed against traditional politicians causing paralysis in the federal government, Republican leaders started to withdraw their support for him, particularly the Senate Majority Leader Mitch McConnell and the Speaker of the House of Representatives, Paul Ryan (with future presidential ambitions) who openly expressed their disagreement with Trump when his actions or statements went a step too far for the establishment to stomach. It is one thing to mount a demagogic campaign to try to win, and quite another to destabilize the system from the very office of President. As for the White House, it turned into a veritable madhouse, where in just a handful of months twelve high-level officials were fired – including three chiefs of cabinet, senior cabinet members, three spokespeople and senior National Security Council staff – by an irascible president incapable of withstanding criticism or differences of opinion. This was as well as having to withdraw, in a matter of days, appointments like Michael Flynn, so-called 'General Crazy', as National Security adviser, when it was made public that he had been on the payroll of Russian state television, had been a consultant to Erdogan, and had lied to the Vice President about his conversations with the Russian ambassador during the election campaign.

Trump responded to all this with scorn, lies and personal attacks, establishing a whole new means of presidential communication: governance by Twitter. He began tweeting his opinions, criticisms and views about any issue or person incessantly, and generally in the middle of the night. Although it might seem to be little more than mindless ranting, it is in keeping with Trump's most important trait: his narcissistic personality. He requires constant adulation and unconditional loyalty. Twice every day at the White House, his aides are expected to bring him articles from the world press where he is mentioned favourably, naturally omitting any criticism. He no longer seeks advice from anyone except his own family members (above all his son-in-law Jared Kushner and his daughter Ivanka) and his most intimate personal circle. He makes decisions and relays them to those responsible for executing them – and later changes them if he encounters any issues that might affect him. When his critics redouble their efforts, he goes back to basics: he gathers thousands of people together in a venue somewhere in his heartlands and harps on about any old topic to draw the applause and fervent affirmation of his unconditional supporters. He is, effectively, always on the campaign trail, because that is where he feels empowered and above all loved – a classic pathological reflex reaction of a grade-A narcissist. On some occasions, such as his rally in Phoenix in August 2017, his speech seems erratic, disjointed and even somewhat delirious, which has caused some commentators to wonder whether he may in fact have a mental health problem, leading some to invoke the twenty-fifth amendment to the Constitution, which provides for the president to be replaced if this is the case. This does not appear likely to happen as the procedure is exceptionally rare and must be overseen by the Senate Leader and the Supreme Court. There are discussions, however, on the possibility of impeachment if the various investigations currently in process were to find evidence of collusion between Russia and his electoral campaign.

In January 2018, his former adviser and confidante Steve Bannon dropped an absolute bombshell that could well destabilize the system even further. In his interview with Michael Wolff for his book *Fire and Fury*, Bannon stated, referring to the investigation by the Special Counsel Robert Mueller, that 'This is all about money laundering', which immediately led to both Congress and Mueller calling him in to give evidence. Why would he say that, and what was he referring to? Perhaps because Bannon is a nationalist who counts Trump's family members among his personal enemies, the couple he calls Javanka (Jared Kushner and his wife Ivanka Trump). He knows that they have long been involved in Russian real estate deals that served as a front for money laundering through investments in Trump's US company, and he maintains that 'Their path to fucking Trump [referring to Mueller's indictment] goes right through Paul Manafort, Don Jr and Jared Kushner'. It goes without saying that Trump severed all ties with Steve Bannon after this statement, and Robert Mercer also fired him from Breitbart News. It seems that Bannon is actually trying to preserve (or perhaps lead) a version of Trumpism without Trump, if past mafia connections and money laundering charges do stick to the president. If the accusations are true, it would explain the sheer proliferation of advisers and contacts in Trump's camp who have links to Russia and the Ukraine, as well as the critical role that 'Javanka' plays in the White House, following years of managing business deals with Russian oligarchs, most notably Lev Leviev and Roman Abramovich, as well as the prominent position enjoyed by Trump's personal lawyer Michael Cohen, with his Ukrainian family and business connections. As an ideologue, Bannon wants to separate the Trump clan's use of the presidency for their personal profit from the movement to transform the political system that he instigated through Trump. The contradiction is that he needs Trump to do this, because he remains the charismatic leader of the 30 per cent of American citizens who still supported him unconditionally, 18 months after his election. Added to this are another 10 per cent of people who support a republican presidency, whoever it may be. From this support base, Trump continues to be the primary political asset for a Republican Party which has been swept up in a radical nationalist movement of white hegemony, profoundly altering the political dynamic of the United States, and therefore the world.

Yet, the fifth and potentially most decisive opposition to Trump and to the attempts to move the country towards ultra-conservative politics, is coming from grassroots movements, particularly from women, from immigrants, from minorities defending their lives against a racist police force, and from young students opposing the gun lobby and Trump's gun-touting followers to claim safety for their schools.

The issue remains that the growing divide in American society is not just a matter of presidential politics. Rather, the rise of Trump is the expression of sharp social conflicts that cannot be processed any longer through the established procedures of liberal democracy.

Brexit

On 23 June 2016, disregarding the recommendations of the main political parties and the Conservative Prime Minister David Cameron, 51.9 per cent of British people (and 54 per cent of English people) voted in a referendum in favour of leaving the European Union, with a record turnout of 72.2 per cent. In 1975, the United Kingdom had voted overwhelmingly in favour of joining the Union, albeit with a much lower turnout. What happened over the course of those four decades to bring about a change so radical that it opened up a deep institutional crisis in Europe and affected the world order? The statistical analysis available in relation to Brexit would suggest that the referendum campaign itself did not have a determining effect on the result; in fact, the majority of the public was highly critical of the negativity expressed by the two opposing sides during the campaign.

The 'remain' camp in particular, in favour of continued membership of the European Union, stirred up what became known as 'Project Fear' by calling on the views of economic and political commentators from across the world who foretold an economic catastrophe if the leave vote triumphed. No such reality ensued. In fact, people tended to react against such voices from the political elites, all of whom banded together in pro-EU unison, which helped Brexit's cause. The popularity of the Prime Minster David Cameron, who had won the 2015 general election with an absolute majority, was counteracted by conservative characters like Boris Johnson, the former Mayor of London and leader of the Eurosceptic contingent within the Conservative Party. The extreme right-wing nationalist party UKIP also played a key role, with its xenophobic leader Nigel Farage who had been successfully elected to the European Parliament a year earlier, swept along by the shameless post-truths peddled by British tabloids like the *Sun* and *Daily Mail*. It is no doubt significant that in the general election that followed Brexit in 2017, UKIP largely sank without trace and not even Nigel Farage won a seat. This was a reflection of the fact that their vote was a purely anti-European protest vote which, after the success of Brexit, gravitated back towards its traditional home in the Conservative Party. This seems to show that broadly speaking, the role of extreme right anti-establishment parties is often to influence traditional parties and pull them towards positions more in line with the evolution of popular opinion. So doing, they are shaping the political decision making from outside the political establishment.

The attitudes that came to the fore with the decision to leave Europe were already present in public opinion some two years ago. The campaign simply galvanized opinions that had already begun to take shape in people's minds, and this seems to be a critical detail when examining the political behaviour of our times. People categorize and assess the information that they receive based on their pre-existing convictions, rooted in the emotions that they feel: electoral deliberation is secondary. This phenomenon was even more acute in the UK, which had always been the EU member state least keen on letting go of sovereignty. There are historical, geographical and institutional roots to this British exceptionalism. The country had long been an exemplar of liberal democracy for many in turbulent Europe, and it tended to set itself apart through the constant assertion of its national interests within the European project. It was in favour of economic integration in order to widen the market available to its competitive companies and leading financial sector, but at the same time it preferred a lower level of political integration so as not to lose autonomy in decision-making. Over many years, therefore, tensions in negotiations between Britain, Brussels and other member states had been managed through concessions to the UK, allowing the country key exceptions to rules: no to the Euro, no to being part of the Schengen area, no to ratifying the EU Charter of Fundamental Rights and systematic objections to the European Community budget. As the arduous process of resolving the challenges of co-sovereignty went on, the negotiated relationship remained the preserve of the British political elites, for the simple reason that its three major parties were all pro-European, save for a minority Eurosceptic faction within the Conservative Party. Everything changed when dissatisfaction with government policies, be they Conservative or Labour, became linked to the country's subordination to the European Union and, more broadly, to the processes of financial globalization, industrial delocalization and rising immigration. To put it another way, things changed when the debate broadened out to include the general public at large, and not just the political classes. The emergence of UKIP (United Kingdom Independence Party) onto the political scene alerted Conservatives to the risk that they would lose their hegemonic control over the more nationalist sectors of society. Hence why a new, younger leader, David Cameron, with aristocratic origins, sought to channel public dissatisfaction in his favour by promising during the 2015 general election campaign that if he won, he would hold a referendum on the country's membership of the EU. This gamble allowed him to displace UKIP and obtain an outright majority, delivering a decisive defeat to Labour and putting an end to Blair's third way or 'New Labour' politics that had attracted the centrist vote to the party in exchange for the loss of its traditional working-class supporter base. In fact, Cameron found himself winning by an even greater margin than he had expected, which meant he had to make good on his election promise of calling the referendum, because he no longer had the moderating influence of any coalition partners. By taking a real gamble on staying within the European Union, he had unleashed forces that he could no longer control. What were these forces?

The watchword: Take Back Control

Brexiteers centred their crusade on a single, fundamental objective, which came to dominate the entire referendum campaign: the British people taking back control of the country's destiny, a reassertion of national sovereignty. It wasn't a reference to imperial nationalism, anchored in nostalgia for Britain's glorious past, but rather a defensive reflex, aiming to protect their right to live in their country, undisturbed. The most direct expression of this attitude was the rejection of European citizens' right to free migration, particularly those from Eastern European countries who had arrived in their hundreds of thousands in the previous decade. Since 2004, and as a result of measures taken by Blair to open up borders to European immigration in line with growing European integration, around 120,000 migrants had arrived in Britain per year, reaching a total of 1,500,000 in 2014. The simple explanation for this was that, according to the principle of free movement of workers within the Union, Eastern European citizens had the right to emigrate and gain access to the same education, health and housing services as British people. In the context of austerity policies and budget cuts following the 2008 financial crisis, this contributed to rising pressure on schools and health services. Curiously, although racism is present in Great Britain, just as anywhere in Europe, this sense of popular rejection did not focus on immigrants from non-European countries, precisely because they needed visas and work permits controlled by the authorities. The Polish plumber was far more threatening than the Pakistani security guard. Taking back control of the country's borders presented itself as the magic solution for eliminating competition in jobs and services and would provide greater protection against global terrorism while they were at it, if you overlooked the fact that most terrorist acts are carried out by people brought up within the country. European immigration became a cipher for the invasion of people's daily lives by globalization in all its forms.

Clearly, then, the explicit reasons that people rallied around the idea of Brexit were greater control of the country's borders and a rejection of immigration. In 2015, support for leaving the European Union was 40 percentage points higher amongst those who felt that immigration was too high than it was amongst people who had no objection to immigrants. What was really being expressed through opposition to immigration and the EU was in fact the profound class and cultural divide that defines British society, and Western societies more generally. The local objected to the global using the only tool at hand: the border. Markets and capital are allowed to cross it by all means, provided that they don't bring people and cultures with them. This basic social division becomes patently clear when we look at exactly who voted for Brexit.

Brexit society
The groups who voted disproportionately to leave the European Union were people older than 65 years of age,

people with lower levels of professional qualifications or education, the industrial working class, white people, and residents of cities and regions that are most distanced from metropolitan centres and Greater London, particularly in the north of England. Sixty-three per cent of those who self-identified as working class voted for Brexit, compared with 44 per cent of the middle class. The Brexit vote among the less-educated sectors of society was 30 percentage points higher than among their more educated counterparts. Men were more anti-European than women, but not to such an extent that gender was a defining factor in the vote. Curiously, areas with lower immigration levels were more pro-Brexit than others; this can be explained by the fact that London and the South East region are home to the greatest concentration of immigrants, the most cosmopolitan and developed area of the country, meaning that competition for jobs and services is not as acute thanks to its relative economic boom. It is also possible that daily contact with immigrants goes some way towards demystifying and dispelling the prejudice at the root of the hostility felt by other native British people.

Conversely, young people, professionals and more-educated sectors of society were all actively opposed to Brexit. The fact is, however, that there is a larger population of over-65 year olds than under-30 year olds, which swung the vote in older people's favour. The outcome of the vote was not only determined by age, but by the level of participation; young people turned out in far fewer numbers than older people, for the simple reason that young people are typically more sceptical of the traditional political parties, all of which were pro-European: the result of this was that young people's futures were left in the hands of older voters. The opposition of class and education level, between those who are equipped to compete on the global stage and those who can only show resistance locally, is captured starkly in the dichotomy between London and the English provinces. London is a global city par excellence, the world's financial capital with one of the most advanced service economies on

the planet. Londoners' capacity for knowledge and information management, key drivers of economic and social
dynamism, is light years ahead of the majority of the country.
Although immigration was the most palpable reason for
the rejection of European integration, resistance to being
dependent on global movements and cosmopolitan culture
is what really lies beneath this, forming the foundations
of Brexit society. Could this be described as a reactionary
attitude? To an extent, yes, because it reacts against the
multidimensional and uncontrolled change that is shaking
our world, from automation to cultural hybridization. That
said, from the perspective of fairness and justice, it is a
reaction that tends to compensate for the dominance of
market forces over people's lives by defending their social
entitlements; it aspires to leverage control over the global
currents that dominate the economy, life and culture by
using traditional state machinery (both national and local)
over which the public do have some influence, i.e. via the
means of their democratic vote. The British elites are able to
consider themselves citizens of Europe and the world, with
open minds and tolerance towards other cultures, precisely
because they hold all the power and wealth within this
system, while the majority of the population, embedded in
their local areas and with not particularly exportable skill
sets, survive in defensive trenches and build their sense of
their lives around their local existence, the only one they
have. So it is that the European Union, constructed without
consulting them since 1975, comes to represent the institutional system that best symbolizes the denationalization of
the state on the idealized altars of European and universal
citizenship, ideals that most people, despite agreeing with
them in theory, can barely participate in in practice.

This is why the Brexit vote was not a class vote in the
traditional sense of the term, but rather a vote by those
who, to use the parlance of the campaign, felt *left behind*
and marginalized by the increasing pace of technological,
economic and institutional change, without a corresponding
evolution in the structures that regulate their lives, via new

forms of representation – quite the opposite in fact. Greater economic and cultural globalization had meant more loss of sovereignty to supranational institutions.

There is, however, a separate and specific case in all this: Scotland. The strong sense of Scottish nationalism, which had brought the Scottish Nationalist Party (SNP) to power and forced a referendum on independence (which was lost by the separatists), promoted a heightened sense of European identity. This is because Europe, in the Scottish context, represents a possible alternative to the supremacy of the British Crown, which is so deeply rooted in the English aristocratic elite. This is partly why Scotland voted against Brexit, including the echelons of popular society which had suffered as a result of the financial crisis and been abandoned by Blair's Labour Party, i.e. people who, outside of Scotland, would have voted for Brexit. In situations where a nationalist sentiment is mobilized, such as in Scotland, the nation prevails over class in the definition of the political project.

Nevertheless, against the backdrop of all these social and cultural divisions, what really determined the pro-Brexit vote in England was the political process that characterized Great Britain in the twenty-first century. In truth, it was less about the referendum campaign itself, than an interaction between society and politics whereby new power relations are expressed.

An anti-establishment movement: from Brexit to Corbyn
Perhaps the most interesting piece of information in examining the sheer extent of the anti-EU movement is this: the Conservatives, Labour and Liberal Democrats all took a pro-remain stance, and yet 40 per cent of Labour voters and 60 per cent of Conservative voters went against the leaders of the three parties to vote for Brexit.

Both electorates were actively engaged in the campaign and turned out to vote, in stark contrast to their tepid support for their parties in general elections, particularly in Labour's case. Blair's strategy of shifting the Labour programme towards social-liberalism (or rather, neo-liberalism with a human face) with the aim of winning over the middle classes, had undermined working-class support, particularly in the industrial regions of the Midlands and the north of England, punished by the results of the economic crisis. Added to this, Blair's defence of the war in Iraq and machinations around it alongside Bush had left his charismatic reputation in tatters, especially among young people. Following the disastrous election result for so-called 'New Labour' in 2015, the reaction from the party's grassroots led Jeremy Corbyn, a veteran left-wing activist, to the party leadership. However, the opposition he faced within his own party's parliamentary group limited his capacity to confront the Conservative Party's policy of austerity. This meant that any voices critical of governments' close ties to the financial elite and the austerity politics imposed by Germany were silenced by a lack of genuine alternatives within the political system. Under these circumstances, membership of the European Union became a locus for protest. In the 2014 European parliamentary elections, the anti-European UKIP Party, with its ultra-nationalist, xenophobic and socially rabble-rousing politics, was the party that received the most votes. When the referendum was finally called, opposition to the unanimously pro-European establishment found an expression for its protest by voting to leave the EU. In other words, two key threads came together in the Brexit vote: opposition for the perceived threat of immigration and the loss of national sovereignty alongside the crisis of legitimacy of the main parties and politics more widely; and a rejection of the austerity politics imposed by the Conservatives and effectively accepted by Labour. When the sections of popular society that did not feel represented by politicians were given a chance to have their say with a decisive vote, they took it. Analysis of the referendum vote shows that the people who voted for Brexit in the hope of having an impact on a specific issue (such as reducing uncontrolled immigration), also hoped it would have a positive effect on all the other problems that they faced (such as the cuts to living standards). It was a protest against the homogeneity of the political and economic establishment on policies related to membership of the European Union.

Having said that, the most extraordinary paradox is that the success of the Eurosceptic Conservative contingent did not lead to a reinforcement of its power, but instead opened up an alternative form of left-wing politics, channelled in part through a reinvigorated Labour Party that put Blairite New Labour politics to bed once and for all and returned to its ideological roots. The Conservatives buried their sparkling pro-European leader David Cameron and named the former Home Secretary Theresa May as Prime Minister. A disciplined woman who had opposed Brexit during the referendum campaign, May was now committed to following through with the decision to leave the EU and took pains to align herself with the party's more radical anti-European wing by appointing Boris Johnson as her Foreign Secretary. But alas, success went to their heads. With the aim of strengthening her negotiating position with the EU, May called a snap general election in 2017, fully expecting Labour to suffer a definitive defeat. Little wonder then that the entire establishment (including leading Labour figures like Tony Blair, Gordon Brown, Jack Straw and Ed Miliband) and the media took to mocking Jeremy Corbyn and his proposals for a Labour programme, branding him an outmoded dinosaur and 'unelectable'. Corbyn, a 68-year-old political stalwart of the traditional left, remained undaunted and stuck to his principles. He proposed selective nation-alization of strategic sectors such as energy and transport, a substantial increase in public spending on education, health, housing and urban policing and the abolition of university tuition fees, all funded by public sector borrowing offset by significant tax rises on the wealthy and big corpo-rations. At the same time, he proposed a limit on top executive salaries to ensure a maximum twenty to one ratio with their employees, and all this without modifying the Brexit decision, but instead advocating for a gradual and negotiated withdrawal from the European Union and some managed regulation of immigration. Weeks before the vote,

May had been ahead in the polls by twenty percentage points, but once underway, the election campaign immediately began to engage the sections of the working class that had been excluded from politics by Blair, along with young people who saw their concerns about equality reflected in the convictions of an honourable, temperate, vegetarian man who won their respect by opposing the political and financial establishment head on. On 8 June 2017, the British political landscape changed, and only a year after Brexit. Labour increased its share of the vote by 9.5 per cent compared to 2015, reaching 40 per cent, very close to the Conservatives' 42.4 per cent share, and they took 31 more seats, wiping out the Conservatives' absolute majority. This time the youth and the more educated voted in greater numbers for Labour than the Conservatives, but so too did working-class voters from industrial areas, returning to the fold of their old social democratic roots. Significantly, a proportion of people who voted for Brexit also voted for Labour, a sign that the pro-Brexit coalition had evaporated as soon as the referendum result was decided and accepted. Anti-immigration Brexit voters split off from those who had voted against the establishment's social policies, and most significantly of all, young people became far more engaged and mobilized than they had during the referendum, with an unprecedented turnout of 64 per cent in the 18–24 age group, which had a decisive impact on Labour's surge. The active participation of ethnic minorities in favour of Labour also contributed to a new parliamentary makeup, with greater representation on the left. In fact, it was only the over-55-year-old Conservative voters that kept May in power and allowed the Conservatives to remain the largest single party, bolstered by the UK's non-proportional electoral system based on seats (non-proportional electoral systems are common in many countries in Europe, even if they don't use the first-past-the-post system as in the UK). Having lost her parliamentary majority, May was able to form a government only by forging an alliance with the extreme right Democratic Unionist Party in Northern Ireland, weakening her position in terms of public opinion and jeopardizing her own political future political in the process. A month after the elections of June 2017, polls gave Labour a six-point lead and their leader Jeremy Corbyn had taken on rock star status among young people ('Ohhhh, Jeremy Corbyn!', they chanted). And so, an anti-establishment movement that had been against the pro-European elites turned into an anti-establishment movement that assembled what was left of the traditional working classes alongside the younger generation who did not see themselves represented by traditional, corseted British politics. The crisis of legitimacy of European institutions, the crisis of legitimacy of the political class and the social crisis arising from austerity politics blended together until the very stability of the social-liberal two-party system that had dominated the last two decades of UK politics was in doubt. Brexit undermined not only European politics, but, in an unexpected and indirect way, the neoliberal consensus of the political class in Britain.

Macronism: the end of political parties in France
The crisis of political legitimacy in France is as pronounced as in most other countries. In 2016–17, surveys showed that 83 per cent of French people did not feel represented by political parties, that 88 per cent of people thought that most politicians were corrupt, and that only 3 per cent believed that governments worked to improve their lives. In what is traditionally one of the most politicized countries in the world, there seem to have been two determining factors behind this crisis of democratic scepticism. Firstly, the economic crisis of 2008 and the austerity politics pursued by governments, with their corollary of three million unemployed, wage freezes and cuts to public services, despite electoral promises. In people's minds, this crisis was associated with globalization, rejected by some 60 per cent of all citizens, in contrast to the 62 per cent of professionals who were in favour of open borders. Secondly, the economic crisis exacerbated a pre-existing political crisis following two disastrous presidencies in succession, one right wing

(Sarkozy) and the other left (Hollande). In his excellent book, Brice Teinturier, the director of the renowned survey company Ipsos, notes how trust in any political option had been eroded by the behaviour of France's presidents and the political class as a whole: Sarkozy's arrogance and contempt for the expectations of the presidential office, and Hollande's indecision and self-flagellation, which he aired to two *Le Monde* journalists in a confessional book which included direct attacks on his own colleagues and lived up to its title: *A President Should Not Say That... (Un président ne devrait pas dire ça...)*. Sarkozy lost the election and Hollande didn't even manage nomination to the Socialist Party primary. The discrediting of the traditional parties, The Republicans (*Les Républicains*) and others in the right-wing block and the Socialist Party (*Parti socialiste*) on the left, prompted a poor turnout in both parties' primaries and a widespread sense of distance from politics. Moreover, the two blocks were tearing themselves apart from within: on the right, the most centrist politician Juppe, clear favourite of the economic class, lost the primary to Fillon, the most conservative of the candidates, who was known for his views against gays and lesbians and who played up his nationalism to court the National Front vote. As for the Socialist Party, against all the odds the left-wing candidate Benoît Hamon beat the incumbent Prime Minister Manuel Valls, who was once an ally of Hollande until betraying him and was known for his repressive, neoliberal politics. So both right and left took a radical position away from their traditional ground. But neither ploy worked. The only sentiment that arose with any force during the pre-electoral campaign was antipathy towards globalization and its consequences, which translated into an upturn in nationalism and anti-European Union feeling. In this context, concern grew for a potential 'Frexit' if Marine Le Pen, leader of the neofascist National Front, were to win the presidential election of May/June 2017. Nonetheless, parallels with Brexit were misplaced. Each time the National Front got closer to power in France, a 'republican' cross-party reaction would always rally during the second round of presidential elections, putting an insurmountable barrier in the way of Le Pen and her acolytes.

In addition to this, however, the leftist tradition in France started to find new modes of expression beyond the divided and discredited Socialist Party, the party of austerity and unemployment (and invariably tainted by some infamous corruption scandal or other, such as when the Budget Minister hid his earnings and justified not having made an income declaration by arguing that he was allergic to bureaucracy), in the first socialist administration for two decades. A socialist dissident, Jean Pierre Mélenchon, launched a presidential bid under the slogan 'France Unbowed' (*la France insoumise*) that was unequivocally left-wing and inspired by the fleeting social movement *Nuit debout*. In this context, faced with the breakdown of the political system and appearing from outside of the left-right paradigm, a character with hardly any political experience tried his luck in a venture that was astonishingly successful and decisively altered the French political landscape. Emmanuel Macron: senior civil servant and finance inspector, Rothschild investment banker, and latterly Minister of Economy in the socialist government of Prime Minister Valls. Finding himself in conflict with Valls, he decided to take advantage of the Socialist Party's division and confusion, stepping down from both the party and his post in government to launch an independent bid for presidency with a year to go until the election. This turned the first round into a four-way race, which Macron won with 24 per cent of the vote, followed by Le Pen with 21 per cent, Fillon (tarnished by personal scandals) on 20 per cent and Mélenchon on 19.6 per cent. The socialists were out of the race with just 6 per cent and right-wing groups were sidelined. The second round, which in France is only contested by the two candidates with the most votes, was effectively a walk in the park for Macron, because the majority of the electorate chose to present a united front against Le Pen. That said, there were many people, particularly from the left, who refused to switch their vote from

Mélenchon to Macron, as they disapproved of his neoliberal policies during his tenure as minister.

Following his election as president, Macron approached the legislative elections of June 2017 with a clear advantage. Amidst the collapse of traditional parties, his party-cum-movement received a flood of converts from politicians looking for a modernizing home, who were joined by hundreds of neophytes, invested in Macron's aura of new politics.

Following the Brexit result, there was such panic surrounding the possibility that a nationalist France could end up sinking the entire European Union project, that Macron was welcomed as the saviour of Europe and immediately courted by Merkel and other leaders. This included Trump, despite the fact that his social media channels had expressed support for Le Pen and tried to vilify Macron during the election. It appeared, on the surface, as if France had managed to contain the explosive populist force that had destabilized democracy, but the real story was quite different. Although liberal democracy did get a reprieve, this was at the expense of the collapse of the political system that had defined France for five decades. The winners in both elections were in fact the abstainers and the Eurosceptics from both the right and the left: in the first round of presidential elections, Macron's 24 per cent of the vote actually translated to 16 per cent of the electorate, while the votes for presidential candidates who demanded a renegotiation of France's relationship with Europe (Le Pen, Mélenchon and other left-wing candidates) represented half of all voters. Then in the legislative elections, the vote that gave Macron's party an overwhelming absolute majority comprised just 15.7 per cent of the electorate, the same as the 16 per cent he had won in the presidential election. In other words, the core voters behind a president who had seemingly been given a plebiscite to govern actually represented just a sixth of the population. Rather than a triumph for Macron's project, the election result was in fact a mass rejection of traditional French parties, the Republicans on the centre-right and the Socialists on the centre-left. This is also clear from the renewed refusal of the majority of citizens to accept that the neo-fascists represent France. France is yet another country where the traditional political system, consumed by corruption and institutional deception, has imploded in the face of the widespread disaffection of a population looking for something different – albeit without any great enthusiasm. The most significant piece of information in this whole affair is the historic level of voter abstention in the June 2017 legislative elections: 51.2 per cent. An electoral system that is designed not to represent but simply to govern can turn a negligible minority of society into an absolute parliamentary majority. If the distribution of seats had been directly proportional to the vote, the result for Macronism would have been 186 seats, while the left would have won 164 and the National Front 85; Macron would have been in a position of minority in parliament. But so what?, respond cynics and political commentators. The seats won according to the established system are what count, but it is this blind pragmatism that divorces politics from society. Given that the will of the people has been so definitively distorted, it is difficult for Macron to address and push through his desired reforms without the support of 84 per cent of the public. After a set of presidential elections in which 49.7 per cent of people voted for parties which questioned the EU in its current form, to go on without making any changes to the process of European integration can only serve to deepen the elite pro-European path of self-destruction which pushes blindly onward, trusting in its institutional capacity to silence popular discontent. Frexit didn't happen because Le Pen is too much of a fascist for any democratic society to accept, and France Unbowed was too immature to pose a genuine, head-on challenge.

Even so, and as Christophe Guilluy points out in his book *The Twilight of Elite France* (*Le crépuscule de la France d'en haut*), shortly before the 2017 elections, the French political and economic elite, fully immersed in globalization, were terrified by the prospect of a potential *marronage* among the popular classes. *Marronage*, or 'maroonage' in English, is a term inherited from the colonial period, used to refer to slaves fleeing to set up their own community. It does not describe direct rebellion, but rather an escape from the system, which seems the greater risk to the maintenance of the globalized hegemonic order. Their fear is not of a direct challenge to democracy by neofascist ideologies that have been delegitimized by history (at least in France), but rather of many sectors of society deserting a democracy that does not represent them, raising the prospect of a tentative search for new forms of representation.

Macron is almost the archetypal model of what the financial and technocratic elites are searching for as a response to the political crisis in Europe. A bright, honest, young leader with a background in both technocratic state-craft (alumnus of the École Nationale d'*Administration*) and global finance (Rothschild), he has energy and ambition, a romantic personal history, and showed no qualms about taking on the Socialist Party where his political career began, or the tired old right-wing politicians who had long represented the interests of big finance. He also has a clear anti-party political stance, although he had to create his own to play by the rules of the game (although he was careful to name it after his own initials, E.M., *En Marche*, the first thing that occurred to his publicists). Of course, following the presidential elections, he adapted it to *La République En Marche!*, thereby even depriving the right (*Les Républicains*) of its titular claim on republicanism. As for the socialists, there was no need to humiliate them because Prime Minister Manuel Valls had already declared them dead and buried, and President Hollande had insinuated it in his infamous book of political self-destruction. From then on, everything was easy: he chose apolitical professionals, untainted by corruption, while simultaneously opening the doors to any palatable fugitives from the traditional parties, thus polishing off the last of their human capital. And to do what? Deliver a programme of economic neoliberalism and political authoritarianism, which seems to be the liberal post-democracy's formula for resistance. In France's case, this meant prioritizing labour reform, otherwise known as making work more precarious and freezing wages. This is the same old short-termist business sector move, which has no empirical evidence to support it and invariably leads to a contraction in demand and lower productivity among temporary workers. Then there was a toughening of authoritarian measures to maintain order, under the pretext of the fight against terrorism. Macron came to the presidency convinced that a fear of terrorism was the breeding ground for the National Front, and that for most of the French population, restricting immigration, keeping a close eye on the Muslim minority (five and a half million people) and giving free rein to the police were necessary measures that would legitimize a leader who was protecting order. On these bases, he planned to breathe new life into France's integration with Europe, overcoming the reservations of French nationalism through a close alliance with Merkel. Ambitious plans for a leader with such a small base of core supporters.

France has always defined itself as a rebel society, up against an impenetrable political system, with parties in patronage and servitude to the state. One month after the historical social movement of May 1968, the mother of all ideological changes, De Gaulle won an absolute majority in an election. But only a year later, he was thwarted by a referendum that forced him to retire. Macron may be too young to realize this, but the voice of the streets cannot simply be drowned out with riot police and PR campaigns. When institutions close ranks to the voiceless, their only means of self-expression is to find new public spaces, made up of social networks and symbolic barricades. In fact, within just one month of his election, Macron lost ten popularity points and various ministers were forced to resign under accusations of corruption (including the influential politician Bayrou, Minister for Justice with responsibility for transparency in politics). By August 2017, his approval ratings had fallen 27 points, to the lowest level of any president three months after election.

The crisis of legitimacy in France toppled traditional political parties and drew what was left of them together around a new leader, heading up a personality-driven movement under the banner of renovation and modernity. This personal leadership oversaw a style of politics which preserved the interests of the elite by containing the dangers of popular insurrection that were stirring among the extreme right and through social movements, generally weak but influential among younger people (e.g. '*Les bonnets rouges*' in Brittany and *Nuit Debout* in Paris). Thirty per cent of young people aged between 18 and 24 voted for Mélenchon in the presidential election, demonstrating the need to open up new channels for institutional political participation in order for citizens to be able to bring under control the corporate and bureaucratic elites. Macron offered the last hope for political stability in a country which was the cradle of republican values in Europe, and which was starting to lose faith in them. The prospects for the future are unclear, but whatever happens, French politics will never be the same again.

The European Disunion
Building a united Europe with a shared economy and institutions has been the most ambitious and visionary political project of the last five decades. Following centuries of enmity, conflicts and atrocious wars, the majority of European countries came together in search of lasting peace and economic prosperity through an alignment of interests within a complex and fragile institutional architecture. It began as a doubly defensive project: against the internal demons that had led to two world wars, and against the Soviet threat, in this case through a strengthening of the Atlantic alliance with the United States. The project was originally posed as a gradual development of synergy between markets and then economies, starting with France, Germany, Italy and the Benelux, and was later expanded step by step until it encompassed 28 countries from every corner of the continent. In reality, at least for those who started it, it

was always a political project, which utilized the economy in order to create an irreversible new continental dynamic that would transcend borders and overcome nationalism. This was the central idea shared by Monnet, Adenauer, Schuman, Mendès-France, De Gasperi and, subsequently, Jacques Delors, Helmut Kohl, Felipe González, Romano Prodi and latterly Angela Merkel. I have not mentioned any English names here, for although Blair was openly pro-European, the United Kingdom always made it clear that it was interested in an economic community, rather than a political one. Historically, its most important relationship was with the United States, and it responded coolly to the hostility of De Gaulle, who saw Europe as an extension of French grandeur. Germany meanwhile, divided and weakened, could only return to the fold of the community of nations through a fervent pro-Europeanism that would eclipse its record of violent nationalism. Paradoxically, Germany's federalist project and British reticence towards the idea of the European Union came together to facilitate, albeit for entirely opposite reasons, the union's decisive expansion to include Eastern European nations. Germany's intention was to recreate its traditional sphere of influence, while the UK correctly calculated that the more countries that joined the EU, the less chance it would have of effective co-governance as a single entity, thus reinforcing each country's national sovereignty. Nonetheless, the Europeanists did manage to achieve increasing economic integration, captured in the Maastricht Treaty and which culminated with the creation of the Euro in 1999, a unique currency considered anomalous by many economists in that it does not fit into a community without a single fiscal policy and without a common banking policy – a high-risk strategy. Federalism's apparent triumph (although the federal project was never made explicit) did have its limits. Only 17 countries adopted the Euro, some refusing it in order to maintain their own monetary sovereignty (UK, Sweden, Denmark), and others because the weakness of their economies wouldn't let them into the club in the first place. The process of political integration, however, did not follow the same pace. When the EU tried to formalize its institutional nature through a Europe-wide Constitution to be ratified by a referendum in every member state, the project had to be abandoned following defeats in France and the Netherlands and staunch resistance from other countries, particularly the UK.

In spite of everything, at the dawn of the twenty-first century, the European Union project had been consolidated far beyond even the most optimistic projections of its visionary founders. When considered as a whole, the EU was the world's largest economy, with a quarter of global GDP; it was an essential node in global financial networks, with London and Frankfurt leading the way over New York/ Chicago, Hong Kong and Tokyo; its welfare states provided a higher standard of living to its populations than any other region on the planet, including the United States; it represented the area with the highest density of scientific and cultural knowledge, as well as scientific and non-military technological research; political democracy and respect for human rights were, in general terms, fully established; overall peace seemed assured, despite the Balkan war; and although social inequality was growing at times, corrective revenue distribution mechanisms ensured a relative equity level that was unparalleled in the rest of world except for in Canada, Australia and New Zealand; and lastly, European ecological awareness and environmental policies were the most advanced in the world, and formed the blue planet's most reliable line of defence. Nevertheless, this construct, built through ideological resolve, did have some serious fault lines running through it that have become apparent over the last ten years, possibly endangering the whole European dream.

There were three main faults inherent in the construction of the European project, according to research carried out between 2012 and 2016 with the participation of 15 prestigious academics from various countries, the results of which are presented in a volume published by Polity Press in 2017, under the title *Europe's Crises*. The first was the

lack of a common European identity, of a strong sense of
shared belonging to a cultural and institutional community.
This is not a trivial issue, because without this common
identity, everything is rosy only when being European has
advantages and no downsides. Crossing borders freely,
paying with the same money, enjoying a larger market and
employment mobility are advantages valued by European
citizens. But the problems start when it comes to digging
deep to resolve the social problems or economic difficulties
of 'other countries'. So where could a common European
identity stem from? Obviously not language or religion
(because its states are secular and home to non-Christian
minority religions), nor from a shared history or territory,
because customs and institutions split up and diversify the
region, nor race, a dangerous notion that cannot unify pluri-
ethnic societies. An identity based on values connected to
civilization, such as liberal democracy or human rights, is
not exclusive to Europe, given that it extends to many other
countries, not least North America and Latin America. So
where does this leave us? A community of identity can have
only two meanings. The first is self-definition through the
exclusion of the other, of those who aren't like us – in other
words, xenophobic distinction. The second, more loaded
with meaning, is the one I have conceptualized in my works
as the 'project-identity', or the will to share a common
project, to want to be Europeans, above national identities,
and to discover what this means through common practice
such as jobs, schooling, politics, culture. It is this project-
identity, to be built through practice, which the European
visionaries were always seeking. To achieve it, however, they
accelerated the integration process without first ensuring it
was embedded in citizens' minds, leaving most people behind
on the way, particularly those with lower education levels
and older people. All studies show that the will towards
the European project is strongest among young people and
highly educated professionals, although even among these
groups it is still in the minority. As such, the cultural basis
for the European construction project was, and still is, very

fragile. In reality, it primarily reflected the culture of the educated, humanist elites who favoured the so-called social market economy and who made peace an absolute priority, along with what they described as European values, which were in fact shared with Western democracies around the world.

This political construction project, serving values identified with civilization, was nonetheless an elitist and technocratic project that was imposed on citizens without debate and with very little consultation. It was a typical example of enlightened despotism ('everything for the people, but without the people'); I don't offer this as a criticism, merely as a statement of fact. Subjectively, I share the ideals that guided the European project. It wasn't simply a case, as the dogmatic left proclaimed, of a reductionist project to create a 'Europe of capital', although countries obviously continued to function as capitalist economies within the European framework. In fact, social democracy was the project's strongest guiding political principle, and countries from the south of the continent (Greece, Spain, Portugal) benefited enormously from their membership of the Union which definitively enabled them to move away from the dangers of authoritarianism and military coups (the last attempted coup took place in Spain just five years before it joined the European Community). That said, the subjection of national sovereignty to legislation and decisions made by the European Commission was never up for debate, and certainly not voted upon. Given that the main parties and the majority of the political class were all pro-European, national elections were of no use to this debate, and European elections, with low levels of voter engagement, were channelled towards a European parliament, which for a long time had no real powers. Even more significantly, as decisions taken by the Commission and the Council of Ministers came to play an increasingly important role in national politics (75 per cent of laws would require some sort of Brussels approval), the Commission had a tendency to act as if it were a European government, and its president the entire EU's president – but they had in fact been handpicked by governments, not elected. Furthermore, while countries did have the right of veto over the Council's deliberations, the clout of the larger countries was always decisive, since they were the main contributors to the European budget and the European Central Bank. This meant that the already considerable distancing of citizens from their national governments was compounded by their even greater distance from European discussion and debate, and that this distance became unbreachable in relation to the daily governance of the technocratic European Commission, propped up by a privileged civil service that was generally maligned by the large majority of the population. Incidentally, this is at odds with my personal experience through my long collaboration with the Commission, of the competence and goodwill of the majority of its civil servants. It was their location within a system built from the top down, rather than through the delegation of power to democratic oversight, which ultimately delegitimized the actions of European institutions. This is the root of the so-called democratic deficit that has corroded the European project.

Lastly, the economic integration process was to a large extent a means of political leverage, enabling European unity to be imposed over the will and awareness of the public. For Germany and France in particular, it was essential that mechanisms were created that would render European unification irreversible, starting with the most obvious: economic integration, which would enable competition on a world stage ruled by globalization. For citizens of many European countries, however, globalization and European integration have come to mean the same thing, tarring both with the same brush.

The key mechanism devised for European integration was the audacious creation of the Euro in 1999. Establishing a common currency for very disparate economies in terms of productivity and competitiveness without corresponding unification of fiscal policy and the banking system was considered potentially self-destructive by many economists,

such as Paul Krugman or Joseph Stiglitz. As already
mentioned, only 17 countries adopted the new currency;
those that did not either wanted to preserve their national
sovereignty or their economies were too weak. Even so,
the Euro gave countries and companies access to limitless
borrowing on a strong currency and it allowed the wealthiest
countries, especially France and Germany, to benefit from
new markets, safe in the knowledge that the risks were
covered by the European Central Bank. But when the
inflated mortgage market bubble burst in the United States
and the crisis spread to Europe in the autumn of 2008,
debt levels became untenable, speculation threatened the
Euro and restrictions on credit and public spending devas-
tated the economy, leading to major unemployment. It
was then that Germany's hegemony over this European
economy, bound together by a common currency, became
clear: suddenly it was in a position to impose budgetary
austerity policies to serve its own interests and those of its
allies in northern Europe, but which damaged the economic
recovery prospects of southern European economies, where
austerity deepened the crisis. European economies, as the
drama of the Greek crisis shows, found themselves with a
dilemma: whether to defend the Euro, subjecting themselves
to the austerity policies devised by Germany, or to leave the
common currency and face the collapse of their financial
system and the massive devaluation of their savings. While I
won't go as far as the great German sociologist Ulrich Beck
did in calling out 'Merkiavellianism', it does seem clear that
the irreversible integration of unequal economies did favour
the most powerful. In fact, pan-European economic policy
during the crisis was dictated by the so-called 'Troika',
made up of the European Central Bank, the European
Commission and the International Monetary Fund, which
became a veritable supranational economic authority with
no democratic oversight. The Troika's technocrats imposed
criteria on each individual country based on its capacity to
provide the resources required for the financial bailout of the
countries and financial institutions closest to collapse. On

the one hand, and in strictly economic terms as David Marsh and Olivier Bouin have analysed, considering the range of member states which could not be compensated through fiscal policies, the Eurozone crisis was effectively prewritten into the common currency's design. This technical defect created a crisis that could only be overcome through the centralization of policies at the European level, which favoured both systemic integration and Germany's hegemony over this process. Although it was not a conscious plan, the northern European countries recognized the potential benefits of this situation for imposing their economic policies onto their disobedient neighbours to the south, suspicious as they were – according to public statements made at the time by the Dutch finance minister – of their wasting aid on 'alcohol and women' (*sic*). This political imposition was resisted by those strong enough to do so – the UK, although it would go on to introduce its own austerity policy – and by millions of European citizens who blamed the European Commission and the Troika for the hardships they were being subjected to, while the banks that had speculated and then later went bankrupt, such as Bankia in Spain, were being bailed out. At the same time, northern European citizens expressed strong criticism about the decision to help the profligate south of the continent, proof of the lack of solidarity between countries and the fragility of the shared project.

The Eurozone crisis demonstrated the disparity between different member states' interests, the distrust between their populations and the domination of financial interests over social priorities in the policies of European institutions. The result was a deepening of the crisis of legitimacy of those institutions, reflected in polls in almost every country – with the notable exception of Germany, which was the only country to emerge stronger from the crisis. The emergence of a 'German Europe', to use the title of Ulrich Beck's book, contradicted the illusion of a 'European Germany' and weakened the European project overall.

The other great crisis that served as testament to the EU's fragility was the migration crisis, with its two distinct intra- and extra-European strands. Firstly, freedom of movement within the EU had led to major population shifts from the less advanced countries towards the more economically dynamic, as people sought to navigate employment issues during the economic crisis. Eastern Europeans emigrated in their millions to the west and north, provoking tensions in job markets and public services in their host countries, as examined in this book's section on Brexit. Secondly, the dramatic exodus of millions of people fleeing from Iraq and Syria to escape atrocious wars resulting from the geopolitics of the major powers in the Middle East, forced the EU to choose between its humanitarian values and the xenophobic refusal of its citizens to show solidarity with fellow humans in desperate straits. Germany, Greece and Italy behaved with dignity, but most members of the union refused to accept the distribution quotas set out by the European Commission. Under the pretext of the terrorist threat, many closed their doors to humanitarian sanctuary, forgetting the times that Europeans had needed and received it from other countries. In fact, it was even worse than this: xenophobia and racism deepened, and divisions opened up between EU countries over reception policies for refugees, even causing disputes about formulae such as payments to Turkey for taking care of the problem, in exchange for relaxing visa requirements for Turkish citizens.

Effectively, when faced with its two greatest crises of the decade, the financial crisis with its origins in the faulty design of the Euro and the migrant crisis, the EU became politically fractured and its conflicts intensified – evidence of the fundamentally precarious nature of the entire project. Every state defended its national interests, and even Germany, which assumed the leadership role in both economic and humanitarian terms, used the opportunity to reinforce its hegemonic position in post-crisis Europe.

These fundamental flaws in the European construct are what threaten its continued existence and undermine the federal project today: Europe lacks a common identity, its political process is defined by its democratic shortcomings and its population is experiencing barely controllable migratory pressures. Added to this is the illusory notion of an economically integrated Europe, bound by a common currency which in order to remain sustainable required a de facto intervention by national economies via supranational bodies, dominated by Germany and its allies. These were the seeds of the European Disunion which find expression in the depth and vehemence of social and electoral reactions against the subjugation of national sovereignty to the EU's institutions.

The Net and the Self

In the opening pages of my trilogy *The Information Age: Economy, Society and Culture* (1996–2000), I set out the contradiction between two tendencies that have been equally instrumental in the construction of our contemporary world. On one side is the formation of worldwide networks which pull together the activities that give structure to all domains of societies. This is the nature of globalization, which consists of global networks comprising the critical elements of finance, the economy, communication, power, science and technology. Any relevant activity anywhere in the world gravitates towards these networks within which power, wealth, culture and communicative capacity are concentrated. The planet's dominant elites follow this logic of networks and interconnect with one another, frequently adopting the provocative moniker of 'citizens of the world'. On the other side are the vast majority of humans who lack the institutional capacity for agency over the programmes that govern these networks. Meaning in their lives comes from specific cultural systems built around a common experience: where they live, their languages, their own unique cultures and histories, ethnic groups, nations or religions. The logic of networks does penetrate these cultural communities, but it cannot dissolve them. As the power system articulated through networks becomes increasingly abstract, people are more likely to defend their right to be by taking refuge in identities that cannot be reduced to dominant rationales. The power of identity stands up to the power of networks. The nation-state constructed within the modern era can find itself caught between these two tendencies, thanks to its internal tension between acting as a node within the global networks where the fate of its peoples are decided, and in representing its citizens who refuse to give up on their historical, geographical and cultural roots, or to lose control over their work. Cosmopolitan people and local people increasingly occupy different dimensions of social practice. Given that in order to be part of the supra-network, the nation-state has to transcend the 'Self', human representation in the democratic political structure based on the community as defined by the nation-state suffers a profound crisis of legitimacy. At calmer times, when the market can manage the economy and people live peacefully, institutional order is perpetuated through routine. But when the automatic preservation of the system (for example, the financial or social protection system) appears to be under the threat of some crisis, people's reflex reaction is to turn to the institutions paid for and chosen by the citizens that they represent. When these institutions do not meet their commitment to protect lives, their very 'representativeness' is called into question and their tendency to serve the interests and values of groups with exclusive access to power is condemned. The political class itself is included in this, in its role as the collective agent for what is perceived as a huge act of deceit.

In the more than two decades that have gone by since this work was published, the opposing tension between globalization and identity has become more acute across the whole world. Representative bodies began to close ranks and isolate themselves from the people they represent, eventually becoming a system primarily concerned with its own survival, as I have documented in my book *Communication Power* (2009). This is the process that underpins every example of specific analyses set out in this book: the democratic state is in institutional and political crisis, and it is down to its inability to navigate the contradictory dynamic between the Net and the Self, between the instrumental agency of our lives and the meaning of our experience. In this situation of structural crisis and institutional lockdown, it is autonomous social movements, as so many times before in history, that are exploring new forms of collective action rooted in the real lives of the people who produce, live, suffer, love and make projects within the fabric of the human experience. In this sense – and in spite of its limitations and disappointments – the recent process of political transformation in Spain offers significant lessons that bear analysis for other countries.

4

SPAIN: SOCIAL MOVEMENTS, THE END OF TWO-PARTY POLITICS AND THE CRISIS OF THE STATE

A fatigued democracy
In the early days of the third millennium, Spain's young democracy was showing signs of premature ageing. Its political system was dominated by the choice between a right-wing party, the People's Party (PP, or *Partido Popular*), an amalgam of Francoism, conservative Catholicism, neoliberalism and criminal networks, and the historic Spanish Socialist Workers' Party (PSOE, or *Partido Socialista Obrero Español*), reconstituted under post-dictatorship democracy as a social democratic party approved by Europe and in strategic alliance with the financial and business elites as part of a process of Spanish modernization. For four decades this imperfect two-party system gave stability to politics in Spain, which throughout history had been run ragged by dramas, shocks and civil wars. It was imperfect because Catalonia and the Basque Country's own brands of nationalism introduced a critical divergence from Spanish nationalism, espoused by both Conservatives and Social Democrats. Additionally, living on in the margins of the system were the remains of a communist party that had been the main agent of anti-Franco resistance, before later dissolving through its own internal contradictions. Beneath this apparent institutional

normality, however, frustrations and tensions were bubbling away that could find no way to the surface. The political system was well and truly hidebound by the constitutional agreements of the transition to democracy, the forming of which had involved the powers that be charging a high price for their renunciation of dictatorial power. The left neutralized the powerful social movements that had been responsible for opening up the fracture in the Francoist state, co-opted the popular movement and the feminist movement and made the worker's movement subordinate to the imperative of tighter fiscal policy and wage restraint. By doing so, it lost the ability to speak for the interests of the working classes, beyond the basic system of institutional representation. The long-hoped-for democracy was effectively reduced to a 'partidocracy'. The two main parties jointly exercised absolute control over institutions and linked with business, which gave free rein to a systemic corruption that linked the illegal funding of political parties to intermediaries taking advantage for their own benefit. According to the Spanish right's historical tradition, the PP was the party that went further to establish networks of corruption amongst its members and within its internal machinery, as has been gradually revealed by a whole litany of judicial proceedings investigating conspiracies and corruption within PP-controlled public offices. That said, at the times and places where PSOE enjoyed a hegemony, they used the same model of merging public and private interests in the name of the party. PSOE's series of scandals and legal cases were exposed by collusive media campaigns that ultimately eroded Felipe González's leadership, despite his standing as the most charismatic and internationally respected political leader in Spanish democracy. Corruption was just part of the way politics was done, without exception among any party that governed state institutions for significant periods of time. In Catalonia, Jordi Pujol, the prophet of the new Catalan identity and a key figure in the political transition, presided over a corruption network organized around CiU (the *Convergència I Unió* coalition), the Catalan nationalist party that ruled for more than two decades, becoming a veritable machine for extortion from companies. This was aggravated by the fact that the presidential family itself formed the crux of the system, led by Marta Ferrusola, wife of the President and self-proclaimed 'Mother Superior'. In summary then, corruption became a systemic feature of Spanish politics, albeit to different degrees depending on the parties, times and areas involved. This phenomenon became more pronounced under the Conservative government of José María Aznar, which, according to statements that have emerged through legal enquiries related to the funding of the PP, effectively set up a parallel accounting structure within the party in order to skim off corporate funds in exchange for favours and contracts.

The lack of trust in parties became even more pronounced at the beginning of the twenty-first century in response to two far-reaching events. The first was the deliberate lie told by Aznar's government in 2004 about who was behind the attack on Atocha station in Madrid, blaming ETA for what was clearly a barbaric attack by Al Qaeda in retaliation for Spain's participation, alongside Bush, in the Iraq war. The exposure of this lie three days before the elections was the determining factor in the PP's electoral defeat and the socialists' return to power in 2004. The second event, of far greater significance, was the economic crisis of 2008–10, which deepened over the years that followed, exacerbated by the incompetent management of Socialist Prime Minister Rodríguez Zapatero, who started off by simply denying that there was any crisis at all, and ended up implementing the austerity policies dictated by the European Central Bank (ECB) and Angela Merkel based on Germany's specific interests. He even managed, in collusion with the PP, to change the Constitution by introducing elements of restrictive fiscal policy into Article 135, in what was one of the most absurd acts in the history of constitutional texts. With the Spanish financial system teetering on the edge of collapse and the country on its way to a bailout by the European Central Bank in exchange for massive cuts to public services, the crisis of political legitimacy transformed into a social crisis, with unprecedented rates of unemployment. Suddenly, in most citizens' minds, political parties – all of them – were corrupt, deceitful, in hock to the banking sector and in thrall to de facto European powers to save the Euro at the cost of diminishing the welfare state. It is in this vacuum of credibility of Spanish democracy that the cry for real democracy arose.

15-M: They don't represent us!
The social movement that began on 15 May (15-M) 2011 in the main squares of Spain's major cities was the most powerful and influential example of protest against the social consequences of the financial crisis of 2008–14 in Europe and the United States. It was a broadly spontaneous movement that was formed among the margins of parties and trade unions, although many activists from the left and the anti-globalization movement also participated. It initially grew out of demonstrations that responded to a call spreading across social networks under the slogan 'Real Democracy, NOW!' This cry was in fact the only real point of common ground shared by the thousands of people who took part in the month-long encampments, peaceful occupations of the liberated urban space. There were demands of all kinds, diverse slogans and utopian aspirations, often expressed with humour and occasionally even a touch of poetry ('It's not a crisis, it's just that I don't love you any more'), but the common thread that held the protest together was the rejection of political parties and institutional politics as representative of the public. The *indignadas* (or 'the indignant'), as the members of the movement dubbed themselves (using the feminine form of the adjective), tried to reinvent democracy through their own practice and an assembly and deliberation infrastructure, which combined debates in the urban public space with constant interaction in the virtual public arena of online networks. They effectively built an autonomous space, a hybrid of the digital and urban realities, as an essential condition for meeting, getting

to know one another and seeking new forms of political relationships and cultural utopia. This enabled a new type of democracy to emerge, distinct from the empty and cynical forms used in institutions that operated outside of public oversight, with negligible respect for the principles they claimed to uphold. In this sense it was an open expression of the crisis of political legitimacy that had been latent in Spain, as in the rest of the world.

This is why 15-M received a majority of popular support (more than two-thirds of the population according to polls) for years. This was in spite of the general feeling that its criticisms and plans for political change were laudable, but would not be achieved because of their wholesale rejection by political parties, institutions and most of the mainstream media. In reality, it did ultimately have a decisive impact on bringing about change to Spanish society and politics. In the context of an economic crisis that had plunged most young people into unemployment, the authorities' decision to prioritize and defend financial institutions to the detriment of people's living conditions was an indictment that made a lasting impression on the public and led to protests and demands for change in many areas of life. Particularly noteworthy was the campaign against unjust evictions carried out by the *Plataforma de los Afectados por las Hipotecas* (Platform for People Affected by Mortgage Foreclosures), which pioneered new forms of social organizations and leadership. The campaign managed to prevent the eviction of hundreds of thousands of people and achieved landmark European and Spanish legal judgments that put a stop to the sheer greed of lenders. Discussions arose out of the movement that emphatically set out the case for values of dignity, gender equality, tolerance and peace throughout society, and above all the prospect of a different life, beyond bureaucracy and the market. Most participants in the movement were under the age of 35, but their influence spread across the entire population, through social networks that were now used by more than two-thirds of citizens, and through its gradual impact on certain media, where journalists echoed the values of humanity and decency, independently of the hostile attitude of their media bosses. The experience of history has shown that when people's minds change, institutions ultimately end up changing too; accordingly, after just four years, the impact of the movement's values and prime movers had transformed the Spanish political landscape.

From the crisis of legitimacy to the new politics

Somewhat paradoxically, however, the first political impact of the movement was the electoral defeat of the socialist party in government and the absolute majority won by the PP, one of the most corrupt and antisocial governments in Europe, in the parliamentary elections of November 2011. It was ever thus; just look at what happened in France in June 1968 following the historic May uprising. Hit by the economic crisis and to some extent alarmed by the social crisis, the public blames the incumbent government and turns to the only available option, which in a two-party system is restricted to 'the other one'. The truth was, this election marked the swan song for two-party politics in Spain.

In fact, the socialist and conservative parties' combined vote share fell from 73.3 per cent in 2011 down to 50.7 per cent in 2015. The decline was especially pronounced for PSOE, which dropped from 43.8 per cent in 2008 to 28.7 per cent in 2011 (under their candidate Rubalcaba), the biggest collapse in the party's history, and then continued to slip to 22.6 per cent in 2016 (under Sánchez, a younger, more progressive leader), losing over one and a half million voters compared to 2011. Meanwhile, the PP lost almost three million votes compared to 2011, putting them at 33 per cent in 2016. As the two main political parties were suffering substantial loss of support, new political actors appeared on the scene. On the right were *Ciudadanos* (Citizens), a small party founded in Catalonia as a Spanish nationalist reaction to Catalan nationalism. They were chosen by the financial elite as the embryonic form of a modern neoliberal right, far more presentable than the ever more corrupt PP. Under the leadership of a charismatic young lawyer employed by Caixabank, the party attracted professionals from the big cities and managed to secure over three million votes, almost the same number as the PP had lost, giving them 13 per cent of the vote share. This meant the right maintained its relative majority, but it was now spread between two different parties. The radical position adopted by Ciudadanos against Catalan nationalism in 2017, which I will go on to analyse later in this chapter, helped it to gain millions of voters, mainly from the PP, as part of a sudden surge in Spanish nationalist feeling. As extreme right nationalism was being reborn in Spain, the left underwent a profound transformation as a direct consequence of 15-M and other social movements: this led to the appearance of what has come to be called *Podemos* and its coalitions. Various aligned interests across the whole Spanish state formed around the Podemos party, groups that emerged from social movements in the various regions, notably Catalonia with the '*comuns*', *Compromis* in Valencia and the *Mareas* in Galicia, as well as a range of local and regional coalitions, and all in spite of their relative youth and inexperience. Podemos was established in January 2014 and had an astounding start in the May 2014 European elections, where it gained 8 per cent of the vote and five MEPs. But the real political change from the left came in the municipal and regional elections in May 2015. The diverse coalitions that had emerged out of 15-M found themselves governing, in coalition with PSOE and Catalan and Basque nationalist parties, the Municipalities of Madrid, Barcelona, Valencia, Zaragoza, La Coruña, Santiago de Compostela, Pamplona and Cádiz, among many others. Their support allowed the socialists to govern in Seville, Valladolid and other cities, and to take the autonomous regional administrations of Valencia, the Balearics, Aragón, Extremadura, Castilla La Mancha, Asturias and Navarra from the PP. With the exceptions of Madrid, Galicia and Castilla-León, the PP lost all its power at a regional level, which had been the institutional bread and butter of its illegal funding. Just four years after 15-M, the new progressive city governments and the left-wing autonomous regional alliances (including the left-wing Catalan nationalist *Esquerra* in Catalonia) changed the Spanish political map. Statistical analysis by Arnau Monterde, presented in the online companion to this book, found a significant spatial correlation between the cities where 15-M erupted with greater intensity in 2011, and the majority vote for the left in the city council elections of 2015.

The results of the general election in December 2015 established the emergence of a new, imperfect four-party system in Spain. The PP remained the party with the most votes on 28.7 per cent, but with no prospects of an absolute majority in future and dependent on other parties to govern. The decline of PSOE took it to just 22 per cent of the vote share, while Podemos and its allies took 20.6 per cent and Ciudadanos secured almost 14 per cent. Although there were some variations depending on the political process in the following months, the CIS survey released in July 2017 (*Centro de Investigaciones Sociológicas* or Centre for Sociological Research) before the crisis in Catalonia, depicted an electoral landscape that was similar to December 2015, with only a slight improvement for PSOE: 28.8 per cent for the PP, 24.9 per cent for PSOE, 20.3 per cent for Unidos Podemos and 14.5 per cent for Ciudadanos. As usual, this does not take into account the specific cases of Catalonia and the Basque Country where nationalist parties held on to their influence. It is important to note, before paying closer attention to the dynamic of the political process, that this four horse race is a direct result of the political system's crisis of legitimacy as a consequence of the economic crisis, public scepticism of traditional politics and, above all, the appearance of new political options that offer hope to disillusioned voters, despite fierce resistance from the establishment, as we shall see. In turn, these changes to political opinion, with direct electoral consequences, are largely due to two factors. The first is the actions of social movements, 15-M most notably, with their criticism of the injustices of the social and political system that really resonated in people's minds. The second is the profound generational change in political behaviour, as described by Jaime Miquel. Essentially, both the PP and PSOE are old peoples' parties. Most of their activists are over 60, and their voters only form the majority in the over-55 age bracket, while people voting for both Podemos and its allies and Ciudadanos are concentrated in the under-45 age groups. In the specific case of Podemos, the younger a population group, the more marked its support for Podemos. Some see this clear age division as a sign of the disappearance of the traditional parties and their replacement by political expressions adapted to new generations. Currently, however, the high life expectancy among older people and their relative demographic weight do restrict the direct effect of generational change on the political system. In reality, the most profound transformation comes from the crisis of representation of the traditional parties, albeit well contained by the inertia of institutions.

From political change to policy change

The pathway from social change to institutional change is via the formation of a government, and this is where the state's institutional bulk and the action of pressure groups really come into play. To begin with, the principle of 'one citizen, one vote' is not actually fulfilled in any democracy except Israel, and still with restrictions for Arab citizens. Electoral laws are decided by the parties in power and tend to reflect conservative bias on the one hand (for example, the rural vote has greater weight than that of the large urban population centres), and a disadvantage for smaller parties on the other, which generally equates to those that have alternative policies, from the right or the left. Thus, the traditional parties have a greater number of seats than their vote share, and this discrepancy is heightened in right-wing parties such as the PP. In non-presidential systems like the Spanish, once parliaments have been constituted, the formation of governments, and ultimately therefore policies, relies on alliances between those with related interests. Unless, of course, a party has an absolute majority, an exceptional situation which is more likely to be due to a crisis between rivals than a single party's true dominance. In 2011, the PP gained their majority as a consequence of people either abstaining or voting to punish a socialist party that had been elected by the left, but had managed the crisis with right-wing policies, condemned by social movements. Yet as the crisis of representation deepens among the public, the relative majorities of traditional parties are shaved down until they can no longer govern without forming alliances, whether through sharing a coalition government or via parliamentary agreements. This is what happened in Spain as a result of the irreversible move from two- to four-party politics. The PP's relative majority following the 2015 elections was so slim that they could not even manage with the support of the new right, rebooted in the form of Ciudadanos. Incidentally, this support could in no way have been unconditional, since Ciudadanos had presented itself as an alternative to the corruption and authoritarianism of the PP, winning over voters from the new middle classes. The political outcome of this decline of the major parties was similar to the situation experienced across much of Europe, in response to the social critique of old parties as a result of the economic crisis. As in other countries, the programme for government favoured by the Spanish political and financial elites was the so-called 'grand coalition' model, similar to Germany and usually under conservative oversight. The greater the risk of new forces contradictory to the prevailing system accessing power, the greater the pressure from de facto European and national powers to form a grand coalition. The typical outcome of this has been a gradual weakening of social democracy, until its near-total disappearance in Greece, Italy and the Netherlands. Pedro Sánchez, the general secretary of PSOE, resisted any kind of alliance with the PP precisely because of this precedent, despite the party's former leader Felipe González asserting his support for such a move. To avoid this deadlock preventing a parliamentary majority, Sánchez attempted to form a double alliance with right and left-wing parties, Ciudadanos and Podemos. This was almost impossible given that their programmes for government were irreconcilable, particularly in relation to the Catalan question. Added to this was the fact that Podemos felt encouraged by having received only 332,000 fewer votes than PSOE (although this translated into a 21-seat difference) and therefore hoped to outstrip them at any new election. This led Podemos to vote against this centre-right alliance in favour of focusing their attentions on upcoming elections. However, the June 2016 elections did not help to resolve the stalemate, as the PP increased its relative majority, PSOE continued to decline and Podemos stagnated, achieving a vote share of just one fifth. All the elections achieved, in fact, was to demonstrate that four-party politics effectively meant paralysis for the political system, unless it led to a new policy of alliances around key axes: left vs. right and old vs. new. In practice, this meant either a broader grand coalition (PP, PSOE, Ciudadanos), or a left-wing alliance (PSOE, Podemos) propped up by the nonparticipation of nationalist parties, particularly the Catalans. This second option drew inspiration from Portugal's experience, which had given the country the political and social stability to emerge from the crisis. Spain's strategic importance within a European Union in a state of crisis was, however, far more significant, and the de facto powers foresaw greater danger if a party that was as clearly opposed to austerity as Podemos were to gain a foothold in government. Cue the financial elites and European powers swooping in to prevent this outcome, with a tripartite strategy: step one was to isolate and discredit Podemos, which was increasingly being seen as an unexpected political threat to the stability of the system. Secondly, it aimed to clip the wings of Ciudadanos such that it would abandon any socially democratic flights of fancy, declare itself neoliberal and put its support behind the PP, albeit with some logical distance, in order to form a solid right-wing block with a chance at government. Above all, however, it was essential for PSOE to limit its leftist ambitions and let the right govern by abstaining from a vote that would see the widely despised Rajoy reinstated as the government's president, rather than forcing a third round of elections. An extraordinary media campaign likened the prospect of third elections to a national catastrophe; the Spanish public had in fact been relatively indifferent to the subject, before eventually succumbing to the ideological onslaught. That said, the mechanisms designed to contain political change suddenly met their match in an unexpected obstacle: the resistance of PSOE's general secretary, Pedro Sánchez, a politician of the new generation who believed in respecting electoral promises. And therein lay the origins of one of the most outrageous political conspiracies in Spain and Europe's recent political history. This is a conspiracy that bears some analysis, because it carries important lessons for understanding the crisis of political legitimacy, as well as some potential routes towards democratic regeneration.

Prelude to the Grand Coalition: Assassination in the Comité Federal

Like other European social democratic parties, PSOE tried to halt its decline by carrying out some internal renovation, failing to realize that its crisis was largely structural as it had abandoned left-wing politics, above all by failing to defend the welfare state during the crisis. Moreover, PSOE's Jacobin centralism and its failure to understand the Catalan issue gradually led to a crisis with its partners in the Socialists' Party of Catalonia (Catalan: *Partit dels Socialistes de Catalunya*), whose voters were increasingly torn between their socialism and Catalonia. According to the data we have available, PSOE would not have won any election apart from the 1982 elections without their seat differential (not the absolute number) compared to the PP in Catalonia. Following the electoral debacles of 2011 and 2014, Alfredo Pérez Rubalcaba, the veteran politician who had stepped in to replace Rodríguez Zapatero to try to plug the leaks that were sinking the socialist boat, finally threw in the towel. The party next tried to reinvent itself by giving activists a direct vote to elect its general secretary, not unlike what happened in the UK Labour Party with Jeremy Corbyn succeeding the Third Way politicians in the leadership. In the PSOE the pro-grand coalition had a candidate. All signs pointed to Susana Díaz, president of the regional government of Andalusia, the largest Socialist Federation, to be the candidate with the support of Felipe González. However, rather than risk her cosy Andalusian seat, Díaz chose to back – for the time being at least – a relatively young candidate, Pedro Sánchez, an economist and university professor, over the parliamentary group's candidate who she regarded as less malleable. As is often the case, Sánchez rapidly began to assert his own personality and political strategy, much to the astonishment of the party machine, which had seen him as a mere transitional leader.

Sánchez rejected an alliance with Rajoy after the 2015 elections, hoping to inspire an alternative majority. The party's old guard advised and practically ordered him to show preference to Ciudadanos, the new right, in any alliance; in no way was he to join forces with Podemos, let alone the Catalan nationalists who were proposing a referendum on independence. In practice, this restricted his actions to a grand coalition, in various guises. Sánchez resisted these pressures and tried to bring Podemos on board with a government alliance, without success in part because of the ideological and tactical intransigence of both Podemos and Ciudadanos alike. A feeling of deep unease spread amongst the Socialist party's historical leaders and their representative on the ground, Andalusia's president Susana Díaz. An alliance of any kind with Podemos or Catalan nationalists was a red line that could not be crossed. Meanwhile, Sánchez was working away to find possible formulas for forming a progressive government that could topple Rajoy in the midst of a bitter internal row triggered by PSOE's autonomous regional barons, who were afraid that resources were to be carved up in favour of Catalonia, to their disadvantage. As the party's power was supported by a network of regional patronage fed by public funds, any loss of the piece of the pie was seen as a threat to its political survival. Amidst gossip and rumours, the deadline for forming a government passed and new elections were held in June 2016, as previously explained. Aware of the anti-Rajoy feeling among the socialist grassroots, Sánchez agreed to the elections with the unequivocal statement that under no circumstances would he support a PP government. Faced with public and private pressures to accept a deal, he coined his now well-known promise 'A no is a no', which was greeted with applause on the campaign trail from a large section of socialist voters who, although distancing themselves from Podemos, were leaning towards a left-wing alliance. Thus, after the elections, the Spanish de facto powers and their representatives in PSOE came head-to-head with Sánchez, the general secretary who wanted his electorate to have the final say. In practice, this effectively meant a choice between three different positions. The first was to maintain the stalemate in the political system, leading to a third round of elections. The second would be for PSOE to abstain from the presidential investiture vote, which would mean it would still be possible for the right's relative majority (through the PP and Ciudadanos) to reinstate Rajoy as president. The third option was to seek an alternative majority that, again, could only happen through an alliance with Podemos and the parliamentary support of the Catalan parties. Sánchez did consider the possibility of this third alternative, although he never managed to formalize this through concrete negotiations; before he could even explore it, a storm erupted within PSOE, led by Susana Díaz and supported by all its former presidents, with the aim of ousting Sánchez from his position as general secretary. What came next was a political conspiracy. On 23 September 2016, according to a reliable account from the Zamora newspaper *La Opinión-El Correo*, Susana Díaz had a secret 12-hour meeting with the PSOE's leading barons from the regional governments, including the Asturian president Javier Fernández and probably Rodríguez Zapatero in the El Ermitaño restaurant close to Benavente (Zamora), to concoct a plan that would force Sánchez to resign, leaving the path clear for the party to abstain from the vote, handing Rajoy the government. The plot was spurred on by various media outlets, particularly the national daily *El País* over which Felipe González, who had said that he felt 'cheated' by Sánchez, had considerable influence. Without going into the details, juicy as they may be, albeit with little relevance to the conspiracy, the important thing to reflect on is why there was such heightened political alarm in Spain and Europe regarding internal PSOE party decision-making. This alarm verged on hysteria, and yet Sánchez hadn't yet even defined the alternative majority proposition in the way that the plotters feared. The explanation for this level of panic can be summed up in one word: fear. Fear of destabilizing the two-party system which existed by common understanding and which formed the basis of the political order in Spain during the post-dictatorship transition – and the ongoing privileges enjoyed by its lead actors. This sense of order was threatened by the new political players who emerged from social movements during the crisis. On the one side were Podemos and its partners, bringing new aspirations to parliament and the major cities, the aspirations of a public that was tired of injustice, corruption and the indifference of those in authority. Cracks were emerging in the control that the de facto powers held over democratic institutions. Elsewhere, there was the Catalan nationalist project, which the social movement for independence had united around a call for a referendum that threatened the very structure of the Spanish state, as I will go on to examine. Even more concerning was the fact that Podemos and its allies supported this request for a binding referendum in Catalonia (although not the outcome of independence itself), thereby amplifying the effects of its political insurgency in the rest of the country. If PSOE was headed for a potential alliance with the people behind this movement for profound institutional change, anything was possible. These fears were founded on a theoretical strategy that had not yet materialized; all Sánchez had done so far was stick to his policy of a 'no is a no' for ethical consistency with his voters, blocking

Rajoy's reinstatement as president. These fears engendered the bizarre coup that ultimately led to the general secretary's political elimination at PSOE's confusing Comité Federal (Federal Committee) meeting on 1 October 2016. In his excellent book *The Ides of October*, PSOE's former political leader and ex-president of the European Parliament Josep Borrell describes and examines the conspiracy, and rather than going into the minutiae of the shameful episode here, I would point the reader towards his analysis. I would only add, to illustrate the fervour of what was and continues to be at play surrounding PSOE, the phrase let slip by Susana Díaz according to a reliable source in reference to Sánchez: 'I want him dead already'. No sooner said than done. But as we now know, the dead can be resurrected through the magical realism of four-party politics, and so the story doesn't end here. To understand this, I must first introduce the fascinating, diverse and dramatic world of the political entity that turned the whole Spanish political system on its head: Podemos.

Once upon a time there was a revolution in the information age
The demands that arose from 15-M were not met with any answers from the Spanish parliament. After various significant demonstrations were repressed by the police, the activists therefore decided to try their hand at institutional politics; as human social crises began appearing everywhere, it became clear that the need for political change was urgent. The European Parliament elections in May 2014 offered an initial opportunity to test out this strategy, thanks to its system of proportional representation. An array of different electoral coalitions formed in various parts of the country. Most of them failed in their bid. Their relative failure could be attributed to the fact that the popular vote, directly inspired by radical opposition to the system, had converged on a newly formed political coalition, Podemos (We Can), which obtained 8% of the vote and five MEPs. Podemos was founded in January 2014 by a group of young academics

based at Madrid's Complutense University Political Science Department. Some, like Pablo Iglesias, Juan Carlos Monedero and Irene Montero, had been members of the Communist Youth Union of Spain (*Juventudes Comunistas*). Others, such as Íñigo Errejón and Carolina Bescansa, came from the anti-globalization movement, and a third group including Miguel Urbán and Teresa Rodríguez had their origins in the Anticapitalist Left (*Izquierda Anticapitalista*). They had all, however, been active participants in the 15-M movement and its later manifestations. They drew up a manifesto and organized online, calling for anyone who wanted to take the social struggle to institutions starting with the European Parliament. They had decided that if they didn't get replies from at least 50,000 people in one month they would abandon the project – they exceeded this target in the first week. And so, without any real means or support apart from the memories of 15-M alive in their collective imagination, they went to the European elections and achieved the aforementioned success. There are three key aspects to Podemos' successful immediate impact, and its later development. Firstly, it benefited from the current of social criticism that had given rise to 15-M, which naturally flowed into the first political project to address the same social issues directly, while also recognizing and respecting the movement's autonomy. Secondly, Podemos made smart and active use of their Internet presence through social networks, the natural space of the younger generations who were most receptive to the message of a new political force, breaking with the traditional parties that had been hit by public distrust. Podemos built a virtual space, Agora, which gave thousands of people modular access to debates and decision-making around its political initiatives. Beyond the actual deliberation hub itself, Podemos coordinated a real cultural guerrilla marketing campaign, on multiple fronts and using multimodal platforms, which helped it to become the go-to political figure in people's minds. This capacity for action in the online arena was no different, however, to the approaches adopted by the other groups that had emerged from 15-M. The true reason for the relative advantage that Podemos had was its communication strategy through traditional media channels, television and radio. Its real added value in this regard was the rhetorical and debating ability of its charismatic leader, Pablo Iglesias, who was a professor of political communications. His image and characteristic ponytail made him extremely popular on TV discussion shows, where he was frequently invited to appear as a guest to provide a counterpoint to the ideological clashes between the usual commentators. In 2003, Pablo Iglesias had also created his own internet television channel, La Tuerka, broadcast via the Iranian-owned Hispasan satellite. It was there that he had produced his programme *Fort Apache*, in which he interviewed personalities from all walks of life, gaining a loyal following among the many people who did not see themselves represented in the dull discussions on tradition channels. Iglesias' media-friendly leadership was the decisive factor in bringing about immediate visibility for Podemos. There is no doubt that this led to an establishment counter-strike to try to destroy his image, with the paradoxical result that the poorer Iglesias' image according to public opinion, the more Podemos progressed in terms of its political influence. Nevertheless, as I analysed in the case of Trump, the media's negative reaction to a personality can lead to constant exposure, exponentially growing their public presence. In a dichotomized and media-dominated world, everything hangs on whether you're in or out, even if the coverage is negative.

There is another important factor that explains the growth and influence of Podemos: its plurinationalism. This is, after all, the reality of Spain, and any political movement that does not reflect it simply reproduces historical structures of dominance, even if they are from the left. This was not an option for Podemos. In fact, it grew out of a number of social movements from Spain's various nationalities and regions, each of which incorporated their own unique cultural identity. The Leninist impulse that is often ascribed to Podemos would have led to it adopting a similar centralism to other parties, including the socialists. But the consultative and partially assembly-based nature of its activism ensured that, in reality, it is not really accurate to refer to one single Podemos, but rather, according to the term favoured by journalists, to 'Podemos and its coalitions'. This term is not fully accurate, given that it is really a confederation of organizations and movements, closer to the anarchist tradition than to the communist model. In no way are *Catalunya en Comú*, *Las Mareas Gallegas* or *Compromis* in Valencia dependants of Podemos. They are autonomous organizations that often adopt their own politics and positions. Rather than a weakness, this authentic diversity, steeped in specific cultures, is in fact one of Podemos' main strengths. By way of proof, the territories where Podemos and 'its coalitions' performed most strongly, in terms of number of votes at the Spanish general elections, were Catalonia and the Basque Country.

The growth of Podemos, in terms of its presence and electoral prospects alike, is a unique case in recent European history: this is an empirical observation, not a value judgement. Just a year after its creation, in January 2015, CIS polls put it in first place in terms of direct voting preferences (i.e., what members of the public say before analysts work their magic on the data). This caused panic to spread among the establishment, left and right. It looked as though a peaceful route towards a revolutionary trans-formation of the state could be opening up, because at the time Podemos really wasn't mincing its words. Politicians were '*la Casta*' (meaning the 'caste'), the European Union was suffocating Spain, and capitalism in its entirety was the enemy. Alarm bells rang and all manner of media and insti-tutional tactics and political dark arts were set in motion, regardless of whether they were lies or slander. The first line of attack was the party's supposed financial and political dependence on Bolivarian Venezuela. It is not the intention here to consider the reality of this connection; suffice to say that the courts which Podemos appealed to did not find any illegality and that the alleged connections were personal to certain leading academics such as Monedero and Errejón, who were political consultants and had given some training to the Venezuela administration for a limited time. Even so, the strategy was effective. The Democratic parties linked Podemos to Venezuelan oil, mirroring what Francoism did to the communists in associating them with Russian gold. A cascade of false accusations and half-truths circulated, alongside direct attacks on Podemos' leaders and key personnel including moves that saw them black-listed by companies and public administrations to deny them employment. Podemos' sense of the viciousness of the system turned out to be right, and they paid the price. Despite this, and following a drop in voting intentions in their favour, they had recovered sufficiently by the May 2015 local elections to be able to build effective city and regional alliances in almost every corner of the country, as previously described. In the first legislative elections after the party was founded in December 2015, they took 20.7 per cent of the vote, and despite being penalized by electoral law, their resulting 69 seats were enough to block both the PP and PSOE from a sufficient majority. Although Ciudadanos did have an impact in a more minor way, Podemos was the catalyst for Spain's two-party system to implode, much to the consternation of the Spanish and European elites.

It was then that problems began to emerge for Podemos, however, as they were confronted with the byzantine process of forming a government through alliances between factions – a far cry from the supportive assembly gatherings in Madrid's Puerta del Sol square. Although I intend to refrain from reciting known facts in this text, I will draw the reader's attention to some aspects that bear general analysis. Rajoy, the PP's leader, was commissioned by the King, as set out in the constitution, to form a government. He counted the votes that he had in parliament, saw that they would not be enough – even with the support of Ciudadanos – and declined. Pedro Sánchez put himself forward, as the leader of the second party, and the King gave him permission to proceed. Suddenly, however, Pablo Iglesias, with his five million plus votes in the bank, appeared before the media and publicly offered to form a joint government with PSOE, with him acting as vice president and various ministerial posts filled by pre-selected Podemos members. This was obviously not the ideal way to negotiate a government and Sánchez didn't exactly jump at the chance. Nonetheless, there was still an opportunity for a left-wing government to be formed with the parliamentary support of the Catalan and Basque parties. As analysed previously, however, pressure from the powers that be (read: the financial elite and European powers) and PSOE's stalwarts forced Pedro Sánchez to include Ciudadanos in any possible alliance, putting paid to the proposed leftist government. This triggered the chain of political manoeuvres that culminated in Rajoy being reinstated in October 2016 thanks to PSOE abstaining from the vote, steered by the team of plotters who gave Pedro Sánchez the push, under instruction from Susana Díaz.

Podemos and PSOE's failed alliance following the first elections contested by the new left did, however, open up a serious debate among the revolutionaries who were destined to become reformists. Should they instead adopt an approach of revolutionary reform, to use André Gorz's classic term, by taking their place within institutions in order to change them? The debate was personified by two leading figures in the movement: Pablo Iglesias and Íñigo Errejón. Barely thirty years old, Errejón had written his doctoral thesis partly at University of California, Los Angeles (UCLA) on national populism in Bolivia. Influenced by Ernesto Laclau's ideas, particularly his notion of empty signifiers, he believed that Podemos should address the entire population as a whole, distancing itself from the left's classic ideas, to allow anybody to project their own aspirations and needs onto a loosely defined political programme. For Errejón, the best way of gradually building hegemony was not to scare people, but rather to make institutional alliances as soon as possible to avoid being isolated in ideological opposition: subtle and strategic, but not in line with the predominant narrative within Podemos, which combined the indignation of 15-M and the Marxist tradition of class struggle, albeit repackaged for the twenty-first century. By contrast, Iglesias wanted to dethrone PSOE, supplanting them as the second party (the so-called *sorpasso*, an old Italian communist concept) and conquering the mainstream for the left as a first step towards leading the process of change. This is why he could not accept a subordinate alliance with the socialists, and even less so when Sánchez, coerced by his party, imposed the involvement of Ciudadanos in an impossible *ménage à trois*. This also explains why, against the views of Errejón and a section of Podemos, Iglesias formed an electoral alliance with the communists of the United Left (*Izquierda Unida* or IU), as a preparatory step towards a potential merger. The equation made arithmetic sense: if the IU's 900,000 plus votes were added to Podemos' five million, they would edge ahead of PSOE's five and a half million. The June 2016 elections would prove this strategy to have been a mistake. One million of those votes were lost to abstention, and Unidos Podemos were left with less that Podemos alone had achieved six months earlier. It was clear that there were communists who didn't want to lose their identity, and citizens mobilized by 15-M who didn't identify with the old left. Podemos took note and began a process of reflection, amidst relentless hounding by the media who clearly saw their chance to destabilize the party's leadership on the basis that Errejón, despite also being a dyed in the wool revolutionary, would divide Podemos. End of story, right? Wrong. Podemos underwent a fast-track development process, updating its internal narrative with the participation of tens of thousands of activists through open online discussions and local assemblies, culminating in a mass gathering in Madrid (known as *Vista Alegre II*) at which they voted on strategy, organization and leadership. Iglesias and his thesis won, with two-thirds of the vote. Errejón responded responsibly: there was no division, a change from the left's typical self-destructive tendency. He continued to take active part in the leadership of Podemos, although naturally somewhat weakened, while his followers saw their sway significantly curtailed. Podemos returned to asserting itself through the popular struggles of streets and workplaces, putting forward parliamentary initiatives that were more symbolic than effective, due to the isolated position they had been left in by a combination of political forces. Even so, and despite being condemned to failure in voting terms, their motion for a vote of no confidence in Rajoy's parliament in June 2017 did have a major impact on public opinion. This was largely thanks to Podemos MP Irene Montero's speech on corruption within the PP, which will live on as a canonical moment in the annals of parliamentary history for its analytical precision and reasoned passion.

The theories debated within Podemos were a reflection of real problems, not merely ideological flights of fancy. Its ability to fit to society would, however, depend partly on how PSOE's leftist trajectory evolved, because if Spanish social democracy chose to step away from the political suicide of the grand coalition and open up to the possibility of a left-wing alternative, this would necessarily in practice involve forming an alliance with Podemos and its allies. Thus, the debate between revolutionaries on possible reformism and the construction of political hegemony was the fruit of the broader political context of a society which could no longer withstand the prevailing corruption, and which rejected a return to a stagnant two-party system.

Beyond neoliberalism: the twenty-first-century left

The most significant change in the renovation of the old parties, both left and right, is that leaders can now be elected, and in particular presidential candidates, by party activists. These aren't primaries in the American sense whereby the general public votes, but it is a process of political appointment that limits the control of political factions as there is always the possibility for the core membership to rebel against the ties of party bureaucracy. It was this ultimate power in the hands of PSOE activists that gave Pedro Sánchez a second chance, against all the odds. Instead of allowing himself to be cowed and disappointed by the brutality of the internal takedown by his fellow party members, including some of his closest colleagues, he reasserted his conviction in left-wing politics and, after several weeks of reflection, decided to fight for re-election as general secretary on a renewed platform, spurred on by the support from the party's grassroots.

I had the privilege of witnessing this period of reflection and final decision-making thanks to one of life's coincidences. Pedro Sánchez wanted to get away from Spain for a few days for some self-reflection, so he headed to California with his family. California has this end-of-the-world aura of exoticism that draws in people from everywhere and anywhere; it occupies the borderlands of human experience, which can give rise to the highest expressions of creative genius, from the technological revolution of Silicon Valley to Hollywood's myth factory that has produced so many of the stories that live in our minds. It just so happens that I spend part of my time there and, having heard about my experience and interest in Spanish socialism, it occurred to Pedro Sánchez that we should sit down and talk about what had happened – and what could happen next. As my friends know only too well, I have a bit of a romantic weakness for the losers of history and lost causes, and so I encouraged him not to give up. If he had, it would spell the end of PSOE, swallowed up in the historical quicksand of the Grand Coalition, that great devourer of European social democracy. We talked and talked, strolling to the soundtrack of the waves breaking on the shore at Santa Monica beach, where I was living. It was clear to me that he had the strength he needed to stand firm and, above all, that he had realized that the progressive politics that he believed in would not be possible without facing up to the de facto powers and the figures within the party who represented them. He knew that he would only be able to do it with the support of the activists, who were appalled by the Socialist leadership's decision to abstain from the Rajoy vote. As I drove him to the airport, there was determination on his face and hope in his eyes. I guess he then honed his strategy

over the coming days. To say it was a long shot would
be an understatement. Almost the entire party machinery
was against him, along with the parliamentary group,
Rajoy's government (which was already licking its lips at
the prospect of the future grand coalition presaged by an
exchange of smiles with Susana Díaz), every former socialist
president, the European powers, the financial elite and the
entirety of the news media, starting with *El País*, the main
Spanish newspaper, which had labelled him with insulting
epithets in a string of openly hostile articles. And if that
wasn't enough, he didn't even have his seat in parliament
anymore, because the first thing he had done was to revoke
his own mandate and resign as a member of parliament, in
order to escape the impasse of either disobeying the party by
voting against Rajoy's reinstatement, or abstaining against
his conscience and his electoral promise. The second thing
he had done was to appear on Spain's most prestigious
political television programme, *Salvados* with Jordi Évole,
to talk about what had been going on behind the scenes
with the parties, including the pressure he had been under
from the powers that be. Commentators had unanimously
cried 'political suicide!', demonstrating how hard it is to
believe that another kind of politics is possible. In reality,
both actions had the opposite effect. In the public's eyes,
Sánchez looked like an honest politician, a rare thing that
was worth applauding. Among the party rank and file,
who smelled something rotten in the decision to abstain
from the vote that handed Rajoy the government, there
was some hope that their party would return to be truly
left-wing, although they hardly dare believe it themselves.
This is where Pedro Sánchez's quest began, visiting socialists
across the length and breadth of the country and connecting
with Socialist local organizations who were resentful of
the party's vengeful new management responding to the
same old dictates. He received significant support from
influential Socialist intellectuals like José Félix Tezanos and
Manuel Escudero, and reopened dialogue with the Catalan
socialists who felt backed into a corner by the central

party's Andalusian leadership, which viewed them as territorial enemies. Sánchez's inconceivable project to rebuild
a social democratic party in the same terminal decline as
its European counterparts, benefited from the inertia and
arrogance of Susana Díaz and her conspiratorial inner
council. They assumed that time would simply heal everything and that party activists would return to the fold as soon
as the memories of the disreputable abstention had begun to
fade. Instead of calling a congress immediately and setting
up a party leadership election before Sánchez had a chance
to catch his breath, they postponed both announcements
for eight months, even delaying the official nomination of
the new leader in waiting, Díaz, long since anointed by the
party's elder statesmen. Andalusia's president did finally
decide to declare her candidacy for the role of Spanish
president and began to prepare for her coronation, hailed
by hundreds of party members and employees and in the
presence of every former socialist president and the mythical
figures of Socialist leaders Felipe González and Alfonso
Guerra. But the interesting thing about politics is that the
process itself can transform the structure of power. That is to
say, what happened during the process of preparing for the
leadership election actually went on to alter its foreseeable
results, and it was an exemplary case of the new forms
of twenty-first-century style politics. Enter José Antonio
González: socialist mayor of the small Granadan city of Jun
and part-time hacker, who had brought innovation to his
town's democracy by introducing direct public participation
through social networks with help from MIT researchers
and the support of Twitter's very own CEO. Highly critical
of Susana Díaz, González designed a system for monitoring
any activity on social networks related to the campaigns
being run by Sánchez and Díaz. By following this information daily, Sánchez was able to gain a decisive information
advantage during the campaign. In fact, it went further than
this, and involves a key detail about the new ways of doing
politics: the election process begins with the prospective
candidates collecting nominations, and the number of

nominations received predetermines the direction of the final vote. Those who make the nomination are named, meaning that the party's machinery has the advantage of intimidation over any dissenting voices. Against all expectations, the evidence suggested that Díaz was receiving fewer nominations than Sánchez, but the really interesting thing was that although Sánchez's followers detected this unexpected trend, they knew that they were being watched closely, and so chose to leak contradictory information. This reassured the socialist establishment into believing that it had overcome the challenge by doubling its rival's number of nominations. When the count was completed Sánchez had in fact obtained more nominations in every part of the country apart from Andalusia, winning a staggering percentage of the vote in Catalonia and Valencia – and by then it was already too late. The Susana Díaz camp had no plan or strategy for this outcome, because it had simply been convinced of her superiority. So it was Sánchez who went on to win the election, comfortably. This led on to success for his programme and his senior personnel in the subsequent congress in June 2017, leaving Díaz to pack her bags and retreat to her palace in Seville, muttering about revenge.

Sánchez's resurrection and victory had three immediate effects on the political landscape. CIS polls in July 2017 showed a remarkable bounce back from PSOE to just four points behind the PP, whose support fell to 28 per cent, affected by the exposure of its corruption within the courts. With Podemos holding steady at 21 per cent, the left's total exceeded the right (PP and Ciudadanos) for the first time. Sánchez then decided to explore possible alliances with Podemos, establishing joint commissions to develop agreements on their programmes for government, ignoring the warnings of the voices demonizing Podemos. Thirdly, Podemos showed that they were receptive to the possibility of an alliance without their previous conditions, and even proposed support for a motion of no confidence put forward by Sánchez. Effectively then, a revitalized Pedro Sánchez defined a renewed socialist strategy, opening the doors to a new kind of left-wing politics in Spain. The seeds of 15-M had now spread further than Podemos, germinating changes in PSOE just as their general secretary had explicitly hoped. New and old ways of doing left-wing politics started to cross-fertilize one another, since twenty-first-century politics will have difficulty to win without twentieth-century roots. The decline of social democratic parties can be reversed provided socially democratic politics are revivified in new social contexts. This is something that most European socialists failed to do, hence their disappearance, and something that Pedro Sánchez was prepared to try, following the transformative experience of his political martyrdom. Yet, the Catalan question, and the dramatic events that followed in October–December 2017 changed everything.

The Catalan question and the crisis of the Spanish state

On 1 October 2017, defying violent police tactics that left 800 people wounded, more than two million Catalan citizens attempted to vote in a referendum on Catalonia's independence, which had been called by the Catalan regional government (*Govern de la Generalitat*) and ruled unlawful by the Constitutional Court of the Spanish government. Of the 2,262,000 recorded votes (43.7 per cent of the census), all cast in precarious conditions given the judicial and police interventions against voting, the immense majority naturally supported the creation of an independent Catalan Republic within the European Union – those who were against the motion for independence hardly bothered to turn out to vote. The PP government, under pressure from Ciudadanos and riding a wave of exultant Spanish patriotism, refused to recognize the referendum, invoking constitutional legality. Despite Catalonia's president, Carles Puigdemont, putting a stop to the application for independence that stemmed from the referendum result, Rajoy issued the Catalan Generalitat with an ultimatum and in due course, having ignored the calls for mediation made by other European leaders, international personalities and even the Catholic Church, the Spanish government suspended Catalonia's autonomous regional status. The government's position was supported by PSOE and its new leader Sánchez (motivated, of course, by their own internal divisions) in exchange for a government commitment to constitutional reform that would revise the territorial structure and organization of the Spanish state. The alliance of PP–Ciudadanos–PSOE was able to circumvent the opposition of Podemos and its allies, as well as the criticisms expressed by Basque and Galician nationalists over the use of such authoritarian measures in an emphatic dismissal of the Catalan people's widely held feelings about their right to decide.

The response from the so-called 'constitutionalist parties', defenders of Spanish unity, to Catalan nationalism was a combination of repression and new elections. On the one hand, at the request of the Chief Public Prosecutor, the justice courts tried and preventatively imprisoned various leaders of nationalist groups and social movements for rebellion, including Oriol Junqueras, the respected leader of *Esquerra Republicana de Catalunya* and vice president of the Catalan government. The legal classification of the crime of 'rebellion', unique in Europe and carrying a penalty of up to thirty years in prison, was applied to a peaceful political and institutional movement which does not stay within the confines of the constitution, precisely because this is what the movement is questioning. Faced with this situation, the president elect of Catalonia Carles Puigdemont and several of his ministers fled in exile to Brussels to claim European mediation to support democratic dialogue between Catalonia and Spain – but without success. It was under these circumstances, with the leadership of the Catalan nationalist movement either in prison or exile, and the Catalan government suspended by Madrid, that new elections were held in Catalonia on 21 December 2017. The Catalan nationalist parties jointly won again the absolute majority of seats in the Catalan parliament, although the party which received the most votes was Ciudadanos, the extreme right Spanish nationalist party, which gained votes from anyone in Catalonia who was against independence. The PP sank because their vote went to Ciudadanos, and Podemos was the biggest loser of all, losing voters in Catalonia and Spain because of its principled political standing that kept asserting Catalonia's right to a referendum while simultaneously advocating talks to ensure Catalonia remained part of Spain. In such a polarized situation, many citizens simply could not understand this nuanced position. Until May 2018, there was no Catalan government in place because the Spanish government refused to allow the Catalan parliament to reinstate the exiled president, despite his having twice won the elections with an absolute majority. Indeed, the Spanish Supreme Court requested the extradition of Puigdemont from Germany. It was a major blunder. The Court of the Lander of Schleswig-Holstein, where Puigdemont was arrested while travelling in Europe, refused to acknowledge the charge of rebellion, and freed the Catalan president on bail. However, because he would be arrested if he were to return to Catalonia, the situation remains at a standstill at the time of this writing in May 2018. The trials and imprisonment of Catalan leaders continue. When you read these words, the conflict is still likely to be underway, in some new guise.

The upshot of this uneven confrontation, the ultimate consequences of which still remain to be seen as I write these pages, has been a deep schism between Catalonia and Spain, in Catalonia and Spain alike. Furthermore, the widespread Spanish nationalist reaction strengthened the support for the most nationalist Spanish party, Ciudadanos. So, nationalism (Spanish nationalism as well as Catalan nationalism), both in Catalonia and in Spain, takes the forefront of the political landscape in line with a broader trend sweeping European democracies.

In fact, a constitutional crisis emerged as a result of the disagreement of Podemos and the Basque and Catalan parties over the proposed recentralization of the state, which calls into question the very system of autonomous governments introduced in 1978–80.

The roots of the Spanish state's 2017 institutional crisis can be found in the original flaws in the 1978 constitution. The constitution was based on negotiations between parties and territories that had been monitored and conditioned by the powers of the Francoist state. These powers were principally the army, a de facto power, and the King, who embodied a project of legitimate post-dictatorship succession, with the objective of relocating the monarchy within the European democratic context.

The negotiation's most significant constitutional flashpoint was the issue of the potential recognition of Spain's diverse national identities and the decentralization of the state through a system of autonomous regions, deemed by some to be egalitarian. The King Solomon-style solution was Article 2 of the constitution, which on the one hand proclaimed the unity of the Spanish nation, while on the other stating that it is comprised of various nationalities and regions. The negotiation significantly managed to make centralist Spanish parties and the armed forces accept the contributions of Basque, Catalan and communist representatives. In exchange, they called for two articles to be included: Article 8, which affirms the role of the Armed Forces as guarantors of the unity of Spain, and Article 155, which invests the central government with the power to suspend any autonomous region which increases its self-governance beyond the boundaries dictated by the constitution. This was the article used to justify the suspension of the Catalan government in 2017. It is no coincidence that the issue of Spain's national identity was of decisive relevance to the democratic transition process; it formed the very basis of the military rebellion that caused the civil war, and went on to become Franco's perennial obsession. The rejection of Catalan and Basque nationalism was an essential factor in the uprising of the armed forces, still tinged with a sense of imperial nostalgia and debilitated by the sad reality of their wretched African colonies. Hardly a surprise then, the protagonist of the uprising was the Colonial Army of Africa, led by the Spanish Legion. Spanish unity was always the unifying principle of Francoism, the nucleus of the fusion between the army and the regime, and the dictator's personal fixation. According to the testimony of King Juan Carlos I, the last words that Franco uttered to him the day before he died, taking him by the hand were: 'Your Highness, the only thing I ask of you all is to preserve the unity of Spain'. The monarch made these words his vocation, and this was the condition imposed on the traditionally republican parties if they wanted to play the political game. Why such fear, almost unique amongst modern European nation-states? Perhaps because Spain was not a typical nation-state, but rather an imperial and theocratic entity that contained a variety of cultures and territories within its orbit, in both its colonies and the peninsula. Although Portugal had achieved its independence following a brief period of Spanish domination, Catalonia's national ambitions had been repressed by force in 1640, 1714, 1934 and 1939.

History does not explain the twenty-first-century crisis, but it is important in helping us to understand the constitutional limits imposed during Spain's democratic transition process. The Spanish transition was lauded across the world at the time as an example of evolution without rupture, but its limitations were gradually revealed over time. What had represented a major progressive leap towards democracy in 1978–80 had become outmoded three decades later, as new generations grow up in a free and democratic European society, in contrast with the Spanish state's age-old authoritarian habits.

For a long time, the marriage of mutual convenience between the Spanish and Catalan political elites progressed without a hitch: it became known as the 'Catalan oasis'. The oasis was the result of astute political opportunism on the part of the Catalan nationalist leader Jordi Pujol, whose party had no qualms in aligning itself with right- or left-wing governments in Madrid in exchange for financial and cultural concessions for Catalonia, as well as for a blind eye being turned to the systemically corrupt practices of his party, *Convergència I Unió*, and the Catalan presidential family's fruitful personal corruption. This clever balancing act was rocked at the beginning of the twenty-first century, as Catalan politics started to become more democratic through the emergence of progressive middle classes who were allied to the Spanish working class, now integrated within Catalonia and with significant power at a municipal level. As a consequence, the nationalist leadership had to be shared with *Esquerra Republicana de Catalunya* (ERC), a party with historic roots, clean in terms of its institutional practices and able to connect with young nationalists, who felt alienated and let down by nationalism's corrupt and conservative nature. In 2005, a bill was drawn up for a Statute of Autonomy that would raise the ceiling of self-governance, while still respecting the limits imposed by Madrid. The statute was approved by the Catalan and later Spanish governments, although it was conveniently diluted in scope and tone in the Spanish parliament. It was finally voted for resoundingly by Catalan citizens in a referendum in 2006. Institutional relations between Catalonia and Spain were very close to reaching a place of stability. But then came 2008–10, when fate seemed to have different ideas.

Three events put paid to this historic opportunity to make Spain a modern and tolerant country, free of Franco's obsession and Juan Carlos I's intimate absolutism. Firstly, the economic crisis brutally shook the country and hit the young particularly hard, and Socialist Prime Minister Rodríguez Zapatero responded by following the German dictate of austerity politics, only making matters worse. Secondly, the PP appealed to the Constitutional Court on the grounds of unconstitutionality, essentially undermining the statute of Catalonia. This was redolent of the historic thread of ideological continuity between Francoism, its successor in the monarchy and the Spanish right-wing made up of the PP and Ciudadanos, a party founded in Catalonia on the basis of a systematic attack on Catalan nationalism. The Constitutional Court's ruling in 2010 crushed Catalan hopes, leaving them feeling deceived and humiliated. It was from this feeling, combined with a sense of indignation about austerity, that a powerful social movement arose, which saw in independence an almost undreamt of chance to start again. Marina Subirats has analysed the 15-M movement against the crisis, what it represented in Spain, and how this sentiment found its expression in Catalonia through an ever more radical movement for independence. Like 15-M (which never actually expressed a stance on independence so as not to divide the movement), the Catalan independence movement was largely spontaneous, although it did centre on two civic and cultural organizations, the *Omnium Cultural*, with its tradition of defending identity, and the *Assemblea Nacional Catalana* (Catalan National Assembly), which united disparate movements around a new, fledgling independence project. Through its political radicalism, the independence movement generated the *Comités de Unidad Popular* (Committees for People's Unity, CUP), a party that was both pro-independence and anti-capitalist, with its grassroots among younger people. The traditional mobilizations and demonstrations that take place every year on *la Diada*, 11 September, Catalonia's national day, offered the perfect opportunity to express the intensity of independence sentiment. Particularly decisive was the demonstration on *la Diada* in 2012, when hundreds of thousands of people across Catalonia descended on the *Palau de la Generalitat* to call for the support of their president, Artur Mas, Pujol's successor. This led to the third ingredient in the birth of the independence movement that would attempt to derail the Spanish state. Mas and his party were profoundly concerned by their declining influence among the Catalan electorate; the Esquerra party seemed to be gaining an increasingly dominant position within nationalism. Meanwhile, Madrid's governments were becoming increasingly radical in their espousal of Spanish nationalism, mirroring the situation in Catalonia, which ruled out a return to the bygone days of forming opportunistic alliances with Spanish parties. While there is no doubting Artur Mas' subjective nationalism, it is clear that this caused a change of tack in his electoral political strategy. Observing the sheer force of the independence movement, Mas and his related Convergencia party decided to step up and lead it. They weren't the instigators of the movement, but they did latch onto its social expression with the intention of channelling it through the electoral system. At first they failed, actually losing votes to the parties that were more unquestionably pro-independence, namely Esquerra and even the CUP, the movement's most uncompromising exponent. From then on, however, the onward march of this new political manifestation of the independence movement carried them on to victory in the Catalan parliamentary elections, although only as part of a pro-independence alliance of various factions, with a programme that promised a declaration of independence within 18 months. This represented a point of no return and was the result of a convergence of factors that were neither planned nor controlled. This is the process that led to Catalonia's attempt at secession, which was met with such force by the Spanish state – for which it was virtually a matter of life and death. Spain never even agreed to negotiate on the most basic issue: the right of a state territory to decide, however much it may plead cultural or historical specificity.

During this decisive period of conflict with the Spanish state, the independence movement took a serious hit when major Catalan businesses decided to up sticks, transferring their headquarters to various other locations in Spain (Caixabank moved to Valencia, Banc Sabadell to Alicante, Gas Natural, Aguas de Barcelona and Planeta to Madrid, etc.). This was a serious blow to the declaration of independence. Viewed from a strictly business perspective, their decision was of course logical as it simply removed any uncertainty. It conjured up, however, the looming spectre of an impoverished Catalonia, isolated from Europe, despite the international public's sympathy for its peaceful, democratic movement.

Although indignation about police repression did elicit solidarity from progressive parties such as Podemos and

Catalunya en Comú which defended Catalonia's right to a referendum, the anti-independence movement picked up pace, both in Catalonia and Spain. The result was a profound sense of social division that made it ever more difficult to continue to confront the intransigent Spanish state, which would defend its unity with every last ounce of its being.

One consequence of the solution of force imposed on the Catalan independence project was the psychological distance it created between the majority of Spanish citizens and most Catalan citizens. It caused a rupture in the basic solidarity of a nation constructed by the state to supersede the true plurinationality of the people coexisting within it. This distance also found its expression in the political sphere; while the new left represented by Podemos and its allies became the defender of Spain's plurinational identity, and of the right to decide of the peoples who made up the Spanish state (be they Catalan, Basque or Galician), the Spanish right dug its heels into Castillian-style centralism, including within this the extreme nationalism of Ciudadanos and the hard right of the PP. As for PSOE, it remained internally torn between the patriotic fervour of its former leaders, represented within the party by the president of Andalusia, and democratic openness to plurinationality. Its general secretary Sánchez tried to stabilize the Spanish state through a proposal for constitutional reforms that would acknowledge its historically multinational identity. But his plan did not find enough support, and he ended up joining the Spanish government in the judicial repression of Catalan nationalism. So, the crisis of political legitimacy in Spain, caused by its democratic failure to be truly socially representative, became linked to the country's inability to represent its different nationalities, whose cultural and historical weight could no longer be ignored and repressed. The current Spanish state, enthroned alongside a monarchy incapable of expressing Spain's multinational reality and undermined by the stain of political corruption, is on the edge of a constitutional precipice, which could jeopardize the very fabric of civic coexistence.

The Spanish experience and the rebuilding of democratic legitimacy

The events of 15-M in Spain were the blueprint and inspiration for networked social movements that spread across Europe, the United States and even Latin America, notably in Brazil and Mexico, as a response to the economic crisis and the collapse of political legitimacy. In some cases, such as Occupy Wall Street, it was the very same American and Spanish activists who had taken part in the encampment at Puerta del Sol square in Madrid who went on to initiate the sit-ins in New York. The social networks behind the Parisian Place de la République movement *Nuit debout* were partly designed by Catalan veterans of social movements called upon by French activists. Movements popped up in multiple countries that had learned from the Spanish camps with which they had direct connections for months. Above all, activists from across the world were now able to embrace the refrain of 'Yes, we can'.

The formation and trajectory of *Podemos* (lit. 'We can') and its political action of taking the social movement into the institutional space, both municipal and parliamentary, is the aspect of the Spanish experience that is most often discussed around the world. Whether in Chile or Mexico, activists are faced with the same challenge and dilemma as the Spanish: how to take part in institutions and change politics without being co-opted by the system. Podemos' journey is being followed closely, and now forms part of the collective imagination of new, younger generations seeking to enact social and political change.

However, the political process is characterized by its relative autonomy vis a vis structural conditions, depending on the actors practices. So, at the time of this writing, in May 2018, a major judicial sentence for corruption against the Partido Popular, the government party, changed the political landscape in Spain. Judging the so-called "Gurtel affair" the court asserted that the PP had created over the years a systemic institutional corruption to finance its campaigns illegally, and that the testimony of the prime minister Rajoy before the court was not credible. In the midst of intense emotion around this unprecedented scandal, Pedro Sanchez, the leader of the socialist party, proposed a vote of non confidence in the parliament. It was immediately supported by Podemos, and after some complex negociations by the Catalan and Basc nationalist parties. As a result, the corrupt government of Mr Rajoy, in spite of the parliamentary support of the right wing party "Ciudadanos", was finally removed from power, and (because of the rules of the Spanish constitution) Pedro Sanchez became prime minister, although supported by a fragile parliamentary coalition. He vowed to remain some time in power, clean up the institutions, enact some emergency legislation to remedy the most dramatic social issues, including financing projects for gender equality, and start a dialogue with the independentist parties in Catalonia. Thereafter, before two years, new elections will be called.

In this context, if Pedro Sánchez would be able to anchor PSOE's position within the left by adapting social democratic politics to modern social conditions and the culture of new generations, this would go some way to creating the basis for overcoming the crisis that is leading European socialism towards extinction as a viable political force. If he succeeds, it would reinforce the possibility of a social democratic renaissance as exemplified by Corbyn in the British Labour movement or Costa in Portuguese socialism.

As for the world at large, in a few cases, we may be seeing the embryonic phase of a process of democratic regeneration, whereby connections are forming between people's criticisms and aspirations and a new political system, permeable to those needs and wishes. In contrast to right-wing populism that has been one response to the crisis of political legitimacy in the US, UK and Eastern Europe, this potential connection between the surviving social democracy and the new parties springing from social movements could be the beginning of an alternative kind of transformative politics, capable of responding to democratic decline with new proposals for political participation, and autonomy from the controlling powers of finance and the media. The possibilities and difficulties of this ongoing process is the lesson to retain from the Spanish experience in the last decade.

5

IN THE SHADY CLARITY OF CHAOS

Not what it could have been:
It is what it was.
And what it was is dead.
Octavio Paz, *Lesson of Things*, 1955

At times of uncertainty, when it's not clear what needs to be said, it is customary to turn to the words of Antonio Gramsci. In particular, his famous assertion that the old order is dying and the new one is yet to be born – which presupposes the necessity of a new order following a crisis. But what it doesn't contemplate is the prospect of chaos. It assumes that a new political order will arise to replace the obsolete liberal democracy which is, quite patently, falling to pieces worldwide, having ceased to exist in the only place where it could really persevere: citizen's minds.

The crisis of this old political order has taken on many different forms. There has been the subversion of democratic institutions by narcissistic leaders who gain the levers of power due to people's weariness with institutional corruption and social injustice; the manipulation of people's frustrated desires by snake oil salesmen and the media; the apparent, fleeting renovation of political representation by the co-opting of projects for change; the consolidation of powerful mobs and fundamentalist theocracies exploiting the geopolitical strategies of world powers; and the return of good-old unfettered state brutality in a large part of the world, from Russia to China, from neo-colonial Africa to neofascist movements in Eastern Europe and the fresh shoots of dictatorships in Latin America. Last but not least is the retreat into political cynicism, disguised as realism, of the vestiges of party politics as a form of representation. The drawn-out death throes of what was once the political order.

The rupture in the institutional relationship between the governing and the governed creates a chaotic situation, which is particularly problematic in the context of the broader evolution of our existence as a species on this blue planet – not least as its very habitability for human life is cast into doubt through our own actions and inability to apply the corrective measures that we know are needed. It is problematic, too, as our extraordinary technological development comes into conflict with our political and ethical underdevelopment, putting our lives into the hands of machines. Then there are the environmental conditions in the megacities that host a growing proportion of the global population, which could cause and are already causing all manner of diseases, while feeding violence. Our planet continues to face the present threat of nuclear holocaust thanks to the madness of leaders with god complexes and no real psychiatric restraint. The technological dimension of new forms of war, including cyberwarfare, could potentially make for conflicts more terrible than their twentieth-century precursors. Meanwhile, international institutions are powerless to put in place survival strategies for the common good, dependent as they are on states (and therefore the short-sighted, corrupt and unscrupulous nature of many of the people who govern them).

Demystifying the ideological notion that institutions are truly representative may well offer us clarity about the world that we live in, but it also leaves us in limbo, unable to make decisions or act because we lack the reliable tools to do so, particularly within the global context where lives are at risk.

The experience of history shows us that from the depths of oppression and desperation, social movements will always emerge in different forms to change minds and thus institutions, just as we have seen with the feminist movement, the rise in environmental awareness and with human rights. That said, we also know that up until now, profound changes have required an institutional changing of the guard to follow on from the changing of minds. Currently, it is at this purely political and institutional level that chaos continues to reign, hence the hope, harboured by millions, for a new kind of politics. But what possible forms could this new politics take? Are we not just facing the same old left-wing trope of waiting for the solution to emerge through the appearance of a new party, the transformative, genuine alternative that this time will finally be the catalyst for human salvation? What if such a party doesn't exist? What if we can't just turn to some force outside of who we are and how we live, beyond our everyday lives? What is this new order that must necessarily exist to replace what is dying? Or could it be that we are in a historically unprecedented situation in which it is us, each one of us, who must assume responsibility for our own lives, the lives of our children and of humankind, without intermediaries, in the practice of the everyday and through the multidimensional nature of our existence? Ah yes, the old utopian vision of self-management. But why not? After all, what's the alternative? Where are these new institutions, worthy of our trust in representing us? I have observed many different societies over the last two decades, and despite appearances, I've not detected many signs of new democratic life. There are some embryonic projects which have my respect and sympathy, principally because I am moved by the sincerity and generosity of so many people, but they aren't stable institutions, proto-parties or pre-states. They are simply humans, acting like humans. They're making use of the capacity for self-communication, deliberation and co-decision-making that is now at our disposal thanks to the Internet Galaxy, and putting this enormous wealth of information and knowledge into practice to help manage our problems. They're rebuilding the fabric of our lives, bottom up, in the personal and social spheres. Is that so utopian? It would be more utopian to believe that the destructive power of current institutions will not be reproduced in any new ones, built in exactly the same mould. Given that the destruction of one state to create another may lead to terror, as we learned in the twentieth century, we could experiment a little and have the historic patience to watch these embryos of freedom, planted in our minds through practices, to see how they grow and transform. Maybe not to build a new order, but rather, perhaps, to configure a creative chaos in which we learn to flow with life's current, instead of forcing it into bureaucracies and programming it into algorithms. Given our historical experience, maybe learning to live in chaos would be less harmful than conforming to the discipline of yet another order.

APPENDIX: HOW TO READ THIS BOOK

The book that you have in your hands, dear reader, is based on a considerable volume of documentation, that I brought together over quite some time in several countries. In order to ease my communication with you, I decided not to include all of these documents and data in the written text of the book, which I wanted to be brief and free from the tedious figures and references that usually accompany my academic work. Nevertheless, I can't think, or for that matter write, without data at hand – it is in my nature as a social scientist. This is why I agreed with my publishers, Alianza and Polity Press, to publish the statistical tables and references on which this work is based on their websites. That way, everybody is happy: my academic perfectionism and I, you who can save time and effort while reading what I have to say, and then anyone who wants to go to the sources can do so online. And we save some trees. An e-book might have been more direct (and that will probably come later), but having spent my life breathing in the smell of paper and feeling the texture of pages, I just couldn't bring myself to make any further concessions. Every one of us is a product of our time, and I am the product of a period of technological transition, hence the printed edition and the website. I must insist, however, that both are integral parts of the book as a whole, a hybrid product characteristic of our communicative transition. A selection of the data that form the basis of this book can be found at politybooks.com/rupture.

I would like to take this opportunity to thank publicly the people who have helped me to review, analyse and sort the data: Arnau Monterde and Pedro Jacobetty at the Universitat Oberta de Catalunya; Sarah Myers and Nahoi Koo at the University of Southern California. My very special thanks go to my personal assistant, Noelia Díaz López, for her painstaking organization of the manuscript and her constant support throughout the preparation and writing of this book.

Lastly, thanks once again to my editor, Belén Urrutia, from Alianza Editorial, and my friend and colleague Professor John Thompson from Polity, who have accompanied and stimulated me on this project, just as they have done with my work for many years.